PREVENTING TEENAGE SUICIDE

PREVENTING TEENAGE SUICIDE
The Living *Alternative Handbook*

By
Polly Joan
Adolescent Outreach Coordinator
Suicide Prevention & Crisis Service
of Tompkins County, New York

 **HUMAN SCIENCES PRESS, INC**.
72 FIFTH AVENUE
NEW YORK, N.Y. 10011

Copyright © 1986 Human Sciences Press, Inc.
72 Fifth Avenue, New York, New York 10011

Printed in the United States of America
987654321

Photography and Poetry ("Milkweed and Me" & "Survival") by Polly Joan

Drawings by Sue Mackay

Photo of author by Janet Fry

Library of Congress Cataloging in Publication Data

Joan, Polly.
    Preventing teenage suicide.

"A program model for guiding adolescents in ways to
understand and cope with depression and/or suicidal
feelings."
    Includes bibliographical references and index.
    1. Youth—Suicidal behavior—Prevention—Study and
teaching. I. Title. [DNLM: 1. Crisis Intervention.
2. Suicide—in adolescence. 3. Suicide—prevention
& control. WM 401 J62p]
    RJ506.S9J63   1985   616.85'8445'088055   84-27872
    ISBN 0-89885-247-1

PREVENTING TEENAGE SUICIDE

The Living *Alternative Handbook*

By
Polly Joan

A Program Model for guiding adolescents in ways to understand and cope with depression and/or suicidal feelings

MILKWEED AND ME

rolling along
on their little legs

like a parachute
they seem to float D
       O
        W
         N
      tumbling on invisible air waves

emerging from their grey papery boats
repeating themselves like an echo
one after another

      filmy masses stick to my fingers
      white clouds streaked with wispy hairs

much looser than I am today
I'm webbed to humdrum
not light and spidery
I'm damp and soggy
my brain is stuck together

yet like these milkweed fairies
I'm lightly hanging on

      anything and anyone
      who stops long enough
      to touch me

Polly Joan

POETRY BY ADOLESCENTS

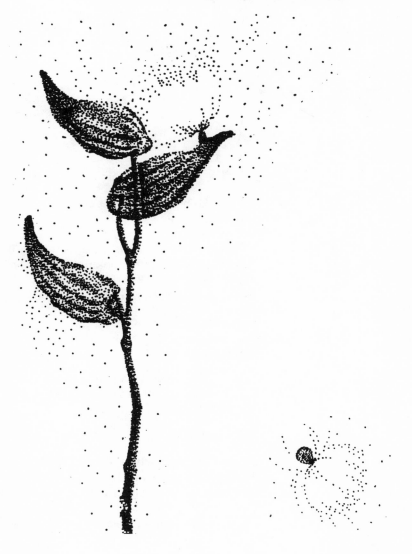

LONELINESS

is like being trapped between
two mountains
no one to talk to
no one to share intimate secrets with
everyone seems to be looking
at you
but they really see right through you

you want to be noticed
but you don't know
how to go about it

everyone seems to tell you
that you don't belong here
and to leave them alone

why do I have to be so lonely?

People are everywhere
but they don't seem
like they want to talk to me . . .

10th grader

DEPRESSION

is like a kite
caught
on a power line
trying to get free

but being battered by the wind

There is no escape.

Winds of confusion
and loneliness
never
        let go

        so down

        a leaf floating
        along the ground

        dark, gloomy
        dead and ragged
        brown
        faded

        almost
        erased

            10th grader

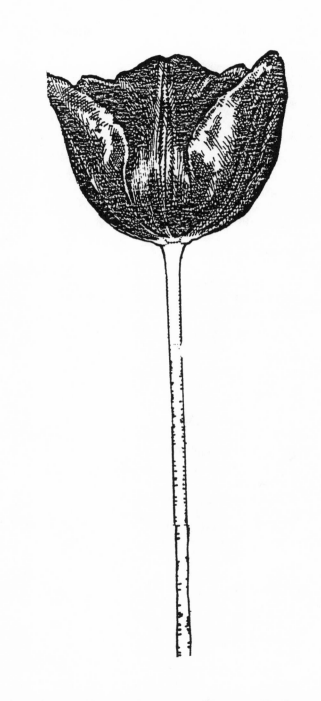

ALONE

Being bummed out is like being in a crowd
being pressed together   everyone wants to know what's wrong
but no one wants to help

It's like being in a crowd with no one to talk to
all in yourself
can't trust anyone   that's what you think

Your friends are no help
and you can't talk to your family
your parents say   Tell me what's wrong

But if you do
you know you've had it
your brothers and sisters just laugh
and don't listen

When you're bummed out
it's better to talk to ones
you're not close to
you can't really hurt them
but they can help you

so tell someone
and feel less alone

17 year old

SPECIAL THANKS TO

All the young people who have shared their lives, their feelings, and themselves with me. It is because of them that I wanted to write this book.

CONTENTS

The Living *Alternative Program*
PART I

Senior High School

FIVE-DAY LIVING ALTERNATIVES PROGRAM

PART II

Junior High School

FOUR-DAY LIVING ALTERNATIVES PROGRAM

INTRODUCTION
Adolescence:
A Need for Understanding

THE *LIVING* ALTERNATIVE is written in response to the tragic rise in teen-age suicide. Adolescents have always tended to reflect most vividly both the strengths and weaknesses of the world into which they are growing. That large numbers of our young people are depressed and feel a sense of hopelessness in any future is a sad reflection on our society's mirrored sense of despair.

The very nature of adolescence is change: a changing body, hormonal changes, changing instincts, fluctuating moods and emotions, and changes in ability to think logically through a plethora of possibilities.

Compounding these difficulties is that society is also in a tremendous state of flux. There are very few givens. Where adolescence has always been a time to question the status quo (almost as a wall to push against), present adult society represents a quagmire of conflicting mores, values, and behaviors. There is no longer an either/or choice for adolescents. The searching, uncertain teenager of the 80s may live with parents who are still working through the 60s and 70s fragmentation of beliefs in traditional roles and institutions.

Feminism and the realization of overt and covert sexism in society has turned understanding of what it is to be a man or woman into angry confusion. Coupled with the renewed search for selfhood of middle-aged adults, the nuclear family too often has turned into an ambivalent battlefield. Between 30 and 60 percent of the teen-age population has had to experience the pain of loss, conflict of loyalty, and guilt of parental divorce.

Also, at a time when the very nature of being an adolescent is characterized by insecurity, transition, and change, many parents are dealing with mid-life transition crises and may be as confused and as ambivalent as their offspring. Parental mid-life crisis, coupled with the complex dynamics in changing concepts of what it means to be a man or woman, mother or father, in this society, has left very few adolescents with a secure and stable home base. Instability and conflict in changed and/or uprooted family patterns are the reasons most often cited for the tragic increase in teenage suicide since 1960.

While possible annihilation through overpopulation, pollution, or nuclear warfare are frightening realities, these threats are more awesome and deepen the hopelessness of the young person in the midst of, or recovering from, family dissolution.

Even the intact family is often dealing with intense internal changes because of the economic situation. These may include working mothers without resources for adequate day care, unemployment and extra jobs taken on by parents to make ends meet, and pressure on young people to work or care for younger siblings. But whatever the complex of problems in the family, some adolescents find themselves taking on the burden of responsibility for these problems. Sometimes a family unconsciously scapegoats another family member as the cause of its problems. The young person who either assumes the responsibility for family problems, or who feels blamed for them, has a tremer.dous burden to carry. The adolescent may feel guilt, conflict, rejection, isolation.

In the midst of this agonizing complexity and without the experience to understand what is happening, a young person may begin to feel there is no way out. A suicide attempt, while a personal cry of despair, can also echo a whole family's deep need of help.

In order to reach out for help, an adolescent may have to expose family secrets such as alcoholism, violence, or sexual victimization. Not only is the young person often afraid of retaliation or at least of further rejection from other family members; but often grows up with a distorted view of what loving and caring mean. In such a household, whether the child is the direct victim or not, the models of behavior observable are confusing and damaging. There is a strong correlation between the intensity of emotional trauma as experienced by the child and the gradual self-perception of the emerging teenager as a worthless and unlovable person.

Further, Drs. Phyllis Topal and Marvin Reznikoff in a recent study point to another cause for adolescent suicidal behavior. ". . . adolescents who feel little control over their environment may experience their families as unavailable, rejecting, or overprotective. Escalating problems could then lead to an increasing sense of helplessness and impotence about effecting solutions within the family, eventually ending in a suicidal mental set."[1]

Whatever the causes, the insecure adolescent deals with a personalized spectrum of anger and/or depression. Without an understanding of the roots of these intense feelings or how to cope with them, there may be a tendency toward escapism. While the need and desire for escape from pain or a feeling of being trapped is understandable, many of the routes taken, such as alcohol and drug abuse, truancy, fighting, petty larceny, thrill-seeking, sexual promiscuity, pregnancy, and running away from home, lead the teenager into problems more overwhelming than any she or he was trying to escape. These escape routes all evidence a certain self-destructive quality and a need for help. The method of flight chosen in suicide attempts and

[1]Topal, P. & Reznikoff, M. (Fordham University). Perceived peer and family relationships, hopelessness and locus of control as factors in adolescent suicide attempts. *Suicide and Life Threatening Behavior*, Vol. 12 (3), Fall 1982, p. 149.

completed suicide is especially tragic; and most of these cases are avoidable.

A suicide attempt is a scream for help. It is also a desperate cry for change. "I don't want to feel this way! I want things to be different."

Until fairly recently, talking about suicide was taboo because of the guilt and the degree of stigma borne by the survivors. In some states it is only within the last decade that suicide has ceased to be a crime. Fortunately, people now are confronting the reality of suicide more directly, honestly, and compassionately. Some of this attitudinal change is a response to the critical need to find ways to prevent adolescent suicide, now the third major cause of teen-age death. In order to provide a classroom model that could reach large numbers of adolescents, the suicide prevention program described in this handbook was developed and since 1980 has been used with junior and senior high school students.

To make some impact on this tragic rise in teen-age suicide, it is imperative that adults working with adolescents, and adolescents themselves, understand the dynamics of suicide, its causes, the complex emotions involved, and methods for coping with suicidal feelings in themselves or in helping others. Much of our teen-age population is dealing with various levels of depression a great deal of the time. The pattern of our life and how we feel about it keynotes our attitudes and actions. When teenagers can take no satisfaction in their lives, they become depressed. How they deal with this depression is basic to their survival. The goal in following the program described in this book is to provide our young people with *skills for living* and to encourage them to reach out for help when they are depressed, are having problems, or are feeling suicidal.

The Living Alternative Program Is Based on the Following Assumptions

While pain and depression are a predictable part of everyone's life at some time, these feelings need not be overpowering. Depression can be a vehicle for growth in the adolescent because it is a signal that something needs changing in the young person's life. The depressed person needs to acknowledge the depression so that he or she can begin to understand its causes. This acknowledgement may be painful, but will enable the personal growth that comes from facing and coping with one's problems.

By facing these painful problems or feelings, one may move from a passive to an active mode, from being helpless to taking control.

Even if the problems are so overwhelming as to be beyond the adolescent's ability to cope with alone, sharing and facing the crisis with others can be empowering and can relieve anxiety until professional help is available.

Design of the Program Model

The *Living* Alternative is designed to provide adult facilitators with content information, teaching methodology, and visual aid suggestions for teaching a unit of four to five sessions on suicide and depression. The program model is flexible enough to be used by public school teachers, nurses, school psychologists, guidance counselors, community crisis intervention personnel, or mental health professionals in a classroom or small group setting. Much thought has been given to providing emotional support and teaching alternatives so that the facilitator can feel secure and confident in presenting this material.

While the program material has been divided into two age groups, one for junior high and the other for senior high school students, all of the junior high material is equally appropriate for older students. One major difference between junior high and senior high school students is that sixteen and seventeen year-olds are not only a higher risk group but also tend to use peers as the major support. Therefore, in the senior high program greater emphasis has been placed on recognizing signs of depression and suicidal clues in order that these young people may be better equipped as rescuers for each other. Also, the dynamics of depression and the emotional factors involved in working through depression is given more in-depth treatment in the senior high program. The emphasis with the junior high group is to help students define their feelings, to understand how the course to suicidal thoughts can develop, and to provide some ways to cope with depression and suicidal attitudes. The program in both groups provides time for practice in listening awareness and an optional final session with an outside speaker. A guest speaker, representing an individual who has been suicidal and is now on the other side, fosters hope in young people. Alternatively, or in addition, the outside speaker can furnish information about community resources where a young person can seek help.

The model has been designed to stimulate thinking and to help students of any age to recognize, identify, and express their actual feelings about living. Some of these feelings are so painful they have been forced down out of the person's own awareness. Talking openly about disappointment, frustration, loss, and rejection may enable some of these feelings to surface. However, since one of the major factors in the development of suicidal behavior is the weight of pain locked inside until it becomes unbearable, the permission-giving of these classroom discussions may be the first step in reaching out for help. Additionally, enabling this kind of discussion can provide an important therapeutic release. *Just to know can help.* Just to know that the feelings an adolescent may be experiencing are legitimate, normal, and that there are things to do about them can relieve the burden.

For both groups, the whole thrust of this program is aimed at supporting young people to seek help, to talk about what they are feeling, to listen to each other, and to take each other's feelings seriously. The program brings into the open the reality and the legitimacy of feeling pain and confirms the very valid human need for understanding and support from others at certain points in our lives. It is not weakness to reach out for help; it is a sign of growing maturity for young people to acknowledge their needs and accept what they require in order to live fully.

Teaching Approach

The teaching approach is that of the facilitator asking students questions in the order suggested. The logic of this sequence is to move the material from factual content toward more in-depth questions that will elicit personal experience from the students. New questions build on information gained from previous answers. Responses given in the program model may be ones students will touch on, but the written responses provide the facilitator with additional material to share.

As an important supplement to the written material and discussion, various activities such as films, role plays, and diagrams are suggested at certain points in the program model. Essentially, the teaching methodology is to create meaningful dialogue between facilitator and adolescents. The facilitator asks questions, gets feedback from students, and then provides clarification, or expanded answers, to these sensitive questions if it seems useful.

The tone in teaching this material may be as much of a message as the content itself, and should be, if the material is to have lasting impact. When the facilitator listens thoughtfully to how the students respond and accepts their answers as honest attempts to meet the questions, this further models the kind of support for nonjudgmental listening that the program seeks to reinforce.

Many young people have had very negative personal experiences in reaching out to adults either in their own families or in their school or community. These experiences may account for "holding it all inside."

However, the pressure of fears of inadequacy, too much anger, longings, and loneliness held inside can build up to the breaking point. In teaching this material, the facilitator has the rare opportunity of providing a listening and caring adult model for adolescents. It is the kind of adult modeling that adolescents can emulate in their interactions with each other.

It is possible that in teaching this material with compassion and warmth the facilitator may rediscover in him or her self some old feelings of pain, loss, and rejection. It is important to realize that this may happen, and for the facilitator to have access to his or her own support network. The reaching-out message we wish to convey to young people applies equally to the facilitator teaching this program.

This is a course about painful feelings. Being honest with young people that as adults we too can be hurt or that sometimes we find it hard to cope models our own humanness. When adults too rigidly hide their pain from young people, adolescents learn to hold this as an ideal of what they should be like. When adolescents can't seem to cope with their own painful feelings, they may feel like failures as well. In contrast, when an adult models strength by truly facing grief or anger, by working through those painful feelings to the other side where hope in living a good life prevails, this fosters optimism in young people.

In opening up some of the adolescent's vulnerable issues, the facilitator may become aware that the young person needs more than the current situation can provide. In order to extend more support if these young people appeal to the facilitator for help, there is a special section at the end of the book on talking with depressed and/or suicidal adolescents. It may be useful to emphasize that the facilitator will probably already feel more competent on these issues, having grappled with them in teaching THE *LIVING* ALTERNATIVE Program.

It is my sense that young people who have experienced this program begin to understand that every human being can hurt, but that there are better alternatives than suicide or other forms of self-destructive behavior. That one must develop skills for living becomes a need taking root. They realize that it is all right for both young people and adults to be honest about how hard it is to cope with some of life's experiences, but that we can get through them.

There are all sorts of personal ways in which a facilitator may make the encounter easier all round. I have touched on my own humanness by bringing my dog into classes and groups. For me, trust and openness with young people seems easier with my dog around to share pet stories with each other: it puts us immediately on the same plane. Also, the presence of that furry body and welcoming paw brings into the room a visible expression of what we all need as an alternative to suicide . . . warmth, confidence, and affection.

Polly Joan

All people appearing in this book are presented as composite characters to protect their privacy.

The Living *Alternative Program*

PART I
Senior High School
FIVE-DAY LIVING ALTERNATIVES PROGRAM

DAY I   GOALS AND MEANS

GOAL   to establish trust between facilitator and students

to create a climate whereby students will feel comfortable about giving honest answers to questions

MEANS   by creating an atmosphere of informality

by listening carefully and nonjudgmentally to student responses

GOAL   to impart knowledge about the causes of depression and suicidal feelings

MEANS   by asking questions, listening to student responses, and by adding informational content where students need a fuller explanation

by developing the "Mountain Concept" on the blackboard (See Junior High Program Model, pages 99 to 106)

GOAL   to begin to understand what to look for as *signs of depression* and *suicidal clues*

MEANS by viewing the film *But Jack Was a Good Driver*

by discussing the film and listing on the blackboard *signs of depression* and *suicidal clues*

END OF CLASS

Reassure class that on the following day students will get some ideas on what to do if they are faced with a depressed or suicidal friend.

Senior High School

DAY I

Is the Suicide Rate Among Adolescents Something to Be Concerned about?

The suicide rate among teenagers has been increasing consistently since 1960. Since that time completed suicides for young people between the ages of fifteen and twenty-four have gone up almost 300 percent. Approximately 5,000 adolescents take their own lives every year; another 50,000–100,000 attempt suicide; and between 200,000 and 300,000 contemplate suicide. At the present time, suicide has become the number three cause of death for adolescents.

What Is the Number One Cause of Death for Adolescents?

Car accidents are listed as the number one cause of death, but many single car accidents are probably impulsive or planned suicides. Since it is generally impossible to prove suicide in these cases, death is usually listed as an accident. If one were

able to list some of these questionable single car accidents as suicide, adolescent suicide might very well turn out to be the number one cause of death for teenagers.

What Is the Cause for this Tragic Rise in Adolescent Suicide?

What are some of the experiences or situations that an adolescent finds overwhelming?

What events at home are too much to deal with?

How has society changed in the last 20 years? Are there different pressures on adolescents? How are these demands or
dreads stronger than a young person can stand up to?

There doesn't seem to be one encompassing reason for this
epidemic increase in adolescent suicide. Teenagers, who should
be the ones most able to answer this question, offer a complex of
reasons related to the changing world in which they live. Those
they cite most often make vague reference to the following: 1)
increased pressure not to fail; 2) more hassles involved with being a teenager; 3) rejection or a sense of loss within the family
structure; 4) disillusionment with planning a career.

On closer scrutiny, these four reasons take on more clarity.

1) Along with what adolescents experience as tremendous
   expectations placed on them to succeed, either in school,
   in sports, at home responsibilities, or in all these, they
   feel that there is less and less leeway for them to make
   mistakes. When young people cannot live up to either
   the expectations they have placed on themselves or
   those with which others are pressuring them, they tend
   to see themselves as failures, worthless and unlovable.

2) Pressures on today's adolescent include the necessity to
   make choices prior generations either never had to face
   or at least did not have to deal with until full adulthood.
   By the very early teens, young people have to find their
   way among conflicting mores related to their sexual activity, their sexuality, and their roles as males or females
   in this society. With the radical breakdown of intact fam-

ilies and disillusionment with institutions and govern-
ments, it is very hard for a young person to know what
or whom to believe in. The tendency is to turn toward
each other, but the attendant peer pressure brings other
kinds of conflict and confusion.

3) Family problems, whether divorce or ongoing intrafam-
ily conflict, can play havoc with a young person's emotions. To the hurt of loss when a parent leaves the
home or when one's secure status in the family is threat-
ened may be added the feeling that the young person is
somehow responsible and guilty for these family problems. Often, adolescents find themselves caught in a
conflict of loyalties between the parents and/or siblings,
pressured to take sides. A young person brought up to
love and respect the family may then feel torn apart.
And increased family conflict is forcing adolescents to
evaluate the desirability of marriage for themselves.
Many are wary of marriage, of having children, doubtful
that they should subject children to what they themselves have gone through. Sometimes an adolescent
takes on the guilt that he or she is somehow responsible
for the family's conflict. In other cases, adolescents can
become the scapegoat for unresolved family problems,
with increased feelings of rejection and alienation from
other family members.

4) While difficulty in getting employment may be contin-
gent upon a society's fluctuating economy, graduating
high school students are facing an uncertain future that
is further beclouded. With the threat of environmental or
nuclear annihilation hanging over young people, many
take a despondent view of forming career choices. There
is a sense of hopelessness in making decisions premised
on a future that may not be. Also, some adolescents absorb guilt for the misery in the world as some young people absorb the guilt for conflicts within a family. When
despair of anything in the world ever getting better is
combined with interpersonal or intrapsychic conflicts, it
can turn suicidal.

Other Causes for Adolescent Suicide

Less often cited as related to suicidal tendencies in teenagers is a family history of alcoholism, battering, or sexual victimization. Young people from such families are always in a bind. They cannot form any constant picture of what love and sharing between people means. They can't go outside for help without betraying their own kin, and fear, making things worse. Accordingly, they have nowhere to go. Thus there is a high correlation between these issues and the development of self-destructive behavior in adolescents.

There is also a notable correlation between emerging suicidal feelings in an adolescent and the previous death of a parent through suicide. Suicidal tendencies are not inherited; however, in families where a parent has committed suicide, young people sometimes look at suicide as a legitimate alternative.

What Are the Feelings of a Suicidal Adolescent?

Suicidal adolescents *hurt*. They feel trapped in a situation where they don't see any way out. They feel hopeless about their lives and helpless to do anything about changing things. In most cases the young person has tried to cope in every way he or she knows with no change in sight. Eventually they turn these despairing feelings back on themselves, coming to believe that all this is happening to them because they are failures, at fault, worthless, and unlovable as persons. Their families and the world would be better off without them. This bitterness may be accompanied by an angry wish to punish those who are left behind. There is an overwhelming loneliness in feeling that no one could possibly understand what they are going through.

How Can an Adolescent Become Suicidal?

By and large there are real and legitimate reasons for painful feelings. The adolescent didn't ask to have these things happen to him or her; it is unfair. In a sense these problems have come from the outside and have been thrust upon the adolescent, so it's a no-win situation. Unresolved miserable circumstances, whether at home or school or both, can trigger depression of varying intensities. Everyone feels depressed now and then, and can even deal with depression over a fairly long period of time without becoming suicidal. However, suicidal feelings can develop in someone who has been undergoing severe depression, a depression which has finally become unbearable.

NOTE TO FACILITATOR:

It is suggested at this juncture to use the "mountain concept" found in Junior High material pages 99-106.

Even developing a modified version of the "mountain concept" on the blackboard will figuratively portray for senior high school students how layering of problems and feelings can lead to depression. The diagram graphically demonstrates how suicidal behavior could be a logical response for some individuals who are experiencing this mountain weight of problems and are feeling helpless to change their situation.

The mountain concept can be a tool for young people to use on their own in attempting to figure out for themselves why they are depressed.

Is Suicide Inevitable if an Adolescent Is Feeling Suicidal?

Crisis intervention can avert most suicides. Tremendous despair and personal loneliness may generate serious thoughts about taking one's own life. Such feelings are terribly frightening to carry around inside. Young people who are suicidal do not want to die; they want to get away from the intense pain. Often just sharing with a sensitive listener can relieve these feelings. With ongoing support and concern from caring people, the adolescent can begin to get some perspective on the problems and discover other ways to change his or her situation.

Adolescents tend to turn to each other for help but often find that their friends do not take their feelings seriously. Most often, one of the difficulties is that adolescents have not lived long enough to have acquired the backlog of experiences which would give them confidence in knowing how to help. Failure to take a suicidal friend's feelings seriously can come out of fear of "blowing it" or "saying the wrong thing."

If young people know more about what causes suicidal feelings, how to recognize when a friend is suicidal, and some ways to help and get help, they will be more likely to take each other's feelings seriously. Consequently, they will be more effective as rescuers for each other.

What Are the Signs that Someone Is Suicidal?

No matter what problems are causing an adolescent to feel suicidal, the signs that he or she is thinking about suicide are quite similar for everyone. The clues to suicidal behavior are logical and reasonably easy to pick up on if one is aware of what to look for.

Film: BUT JACK WAS A GOOD DRIVER

Synopsis: The film centers around a discussion between Ed and Bob, two high-school students, as they leave the funeral of their friend Jack, who has died in a one-car accident. Bob questions whether the accident was really accidental: Jack was too good a driver; it had been a sunny day; perhaps the skid marks were there, not because he'd been going too fast to make the curve, but because at the last moment he'd changed his mind about going off the cliff. Ed is at first skeptical, but as they compare notes, he begins to share Bob's doubts.

They remember things they knew about Jack: that for some reason, he had always seemed to be getting hurt; that he had always pushed himself hard and didn't seem to feel he'd done well enough, even when he won at something; that his home seemed too neat and clean and his parents too formal and cold. They remember that Jack had seemed more quiet and moody in the past few months, and they begin to put together all the clues that indicated things had not been going too well for Jack recently. Bob knew Jack's grades had been dropping—his biology midterm with an F on it had been in a stack of records Jack had returned to Bob. The previous Saturday Jack had given Bob his Nikon —a camera Bob had been trying to buy from him for over a year—and said he was losing interest in things. And Saturday night at the drive-in, he had been turned off by the comedy—he said it was only funny when you couldn't hear the voices. Afterwards, when everyone was talking about what they wanted to do after graduation, he'd said he didn't want to do anything, that, in fact, he had sometimes thought about killing himself and that he couldn't see any reason not to.

Ed at first argues that it couldn't have been suicide— that there was no note (or was there?), that lots of people have mothers who are always running around cleaning up but that doesn't mean they're going to do away with themselves; that he, too, sometimes played with the idea of killing himself but that doesn't mean he ever thought about it seriously; that just because a guy is depressed doesn't mean he's going to kill himself. However, by the end of the film, he's the one who has tears in his eyes and who is feeling uncomfortable about facing Jack's parents. They are haunted by the thought that perhaps Jack had been trying to tell them something in the past two weeks and that perhaps, if they had been more sensitive to his feelings, they might have been able to help him.

NOTE TO FACILITATOR:

As a prelude to showing this film suggest to students that they watch with an ear to picking up on both signs of depression as well as suicidal clues. Friends, sometimes even more than family members, are likely to be the ones to notice shifts in behavior or conversational clues indicating severe depression and/or suicidal intent.

After the film, elicit responses as to what the students think were clues that Jack has been depressed and that his death was a probable suicide. Using the blackboard, list in separate columns Signs of Depression *and* Suicidal Clues. *This will allow students to come up with signs for either column in random order.*

Signs of Depression	Suicidal Clues
1) *Change in school grades*	1) *Talking about killing oneself*
2) *Withdrawal or moodiness*	2) *Talking about "not being" or*
3) *Accident proneness*	*considering any future*
4) *Change in eating or sleeping*	3) *Giving away prized posses-*
habits	*sions*
5) *Other significant changes in*	
usual behavior	

What Are Signs of Depression in the Film?

Change in School Grades

A downward shift in school grades is an important indicator of depression. By and large students maintain a certain performance level in school. When a person is depressed, it becomes very difficult to concentrate. If a student is trying not to think about the problems causing the depression, he or she may not be able to concentrate anywhere else. The person may try to study, may even set up specific times to work and then find the material is just not being absorbed. This can increase one's sense of failure and worthlessness. "What's wrong with me? I can't even do simple homework."

Withdrawal or Moodiness

Often people who are ridden with problems, situations, or personal losses that appear to have no resolution will withdraw into themselves. Life appears to have lost joy and meaning. There is a tendency to spend more time alone and less time with friends "so as not to spoil everyone else's fun" or because being with people who are having fun only underscores how unhappy the depressed person is feeling.

Friends often misread this withdrawal as rejection, feel some resentment, and may back off from the depressed person. This backing off in turn simply reinforces the depressed person's growing feelings of worthlessness. In the increased isolation and alienation from all individuals who could help relieve the depression, the person may begin to ask "Why bother?" "Why stick around if I have to feel this way?" "What's the use of living?" "Nobody cares!" "People would be better off without me around."

Accident Proneness

People who are depressed sometimes physically overextend themselves in self-destructive ways and/or take risks because at some level they don't care what happens to them.

Conversely, depressed individuals may try to be careful, but find themselves bumping into doors, falling down curbs or stairs, because they can't keep their mind on what they are doing.

While being accident-prone is not necessarily a sign of depression, if it is coupled with other shifts in normal behavior, it can be a significant cause for concern.

Additional Signs of Depression Not Included in the Film

Pronounced Change in Eating or Sleeping Habits

Depression usually affects patterns in eating and sleeping. It may become hard to fall asleep or the individual may wake early and be unable to go back to sleep. Depression may also have the opposite effect, with the individual constantly falling asleep, whether at school or at home. There may be fatigue even when the person is sleeping a great deal. Patterns in eating may also be affected. Individuals may almost totally lose their appetite or find themselves eating compulsively. In either case, adolescents unfamiliar with the fact that depression can effect changes in both eating and sleeping patterns may become concerned that now they have even more problems to deal with. This anxiety may increase the depression so their situation seems to spiral into more and more layers of unsolvable problems.

Any Other Significant Change in Usual Behavior

Any change in a person's normal way of acting, which seems to continue day after day, can be indication of depression. Such changes might include getting into a lot of trouble at school, becoming quarrelsome, laughing at things that aren't funny, or responding with tears to situations that wouldn't ordinarily elicit sadness.

What Are the Signs of Suicidal Behavior in the Film?

Like most other people who become suicidal, adolescents really do not want to kill themselves; they just want to escape from the pain they are experiencing and they don't see any other way out. Yet even with acute despair, there is always ambivalence about dying. That is why suicidal people throw out clues which, if taken seriously, might bring them help. At the same time their uncertainty about whether to live or die may be expressed by angry outbursts such as "Don't help me!" "There is no other way!" "Don't tell anyone!"

Talking about Killing Oneself

People who are talking about killing themselves are thinking about suicide. It is important to take this kind of information very seriously even though one might hear such comments in a situation where one is supposed to be having a good time. Thinking about suicide is terrifying for a person. Life is precious and dying is a fearful prospect. It is hard to talk about one's suicidal feelings, both because it is scary to admit out loud that one is thinking about dying, and also because there is fear one will be laughed at by friends or considered crazy or just attempting to get more attention.

In the context of a party or when one's tongue has been slightly loosened by alcohol, it may seem less threatening to talk about suicide. However, almost any context could be the personal trigger for divulging suicidal feelings, such as a quiet talk with a friend.

Talking about "Not Being," or Not Considering Any Future

Talking about "not *being*" (Jack said, "I don't want to *be* anything") or negating any sense of future as in "There's nothing to look forward to," "There's no point in making any plans" are indirect ways of expressing hopelessness about living. Without intervention, these attitudes may crystallize into serious self-destructive behavior.

Giving Away Prized Possessions

This clue usually indicates that the person has made a decision to die and is getting affairs in order. With friends, one usually knows what personal possessions are the most important. When these possessions are given away, accompanied by statements such as "Please take care of this," "I want you to have this," "I won't be needing this anymore," it can be seen as a last will and testament as well as a last-ditch desperate cry for help.

Even though the young person has made a decision to die, the giving away of personal possessions prior to a suicide attempt represents an ongoing inner struggle of wanting someone to find some reason for him/her to keep on living, of wanting rescue before death becomes inevitable.

Other Factors to Consider When Trying to Assess the Lethality of a Friend's Suicidal Feelings

Probably everyone at some low point in his/her life will have thoughts of suicide. Fleeting thoughts of suicide are not uncommon, but the power of these feelings at a given moment may make the difference between life and death.

Teenagers have a less developed sense of impulse control than adults. They are also prone to dramatic mood changes. Life can be wonderful one minute and horrible the next. Without emotional experience and maturation to know how to deal with crises, they may impulsively make a suicide attempt in a sudden shift of mood. This means that early detection of other factors that could be influencing an adolescent's daily life are very important.

If a young person has recently suffered a loss such as the breakup of a relationship, it may seem like the end of the world. A recent loss may also call up feelings left over from former losses: the earlier death of a parent or sibling, loss through parental divorce. In the latter case, adolescents can become overwhelmed with a sense of double loss. At the same time, they may be unaware that the reason the present situation feels so unbearable may be because other losses have re-entered their emotional sphere. Like ghosts slipping out of a closet, losses from the past can magnify the present suffering to unmanageable proportions. The adolescent can begin to feel out of control and entrapped, terribly lonely and full of incurable pain.

On the other hand, when a teenager has endured an ongoing sense of worthlessness, almost *any* sudden loss or performance failure, such as "blowing" an exam, or having a date not show, may trigger an impulsive suicidal act, if the adolescent has been feeling suicidal.

Also, if the adolescent has made a previous suicide attempt, the possibility of suicide as a way to handle pain has already been tried. Many completed suicides are by people who have made prior attempts to kill themselves. Therefore, a person who has made a previous attempt and whose cry for help was largely unnoticed at the time or whose act was ignored as simply an "attention-getter" might very well make another attempt. Succeeding attempts usually increase in lethality.

For that reason, in assessing the lethality of the situation it is important to find out whether the person has considered suicide previously, has determined on a method for suicide and/or has in his or her possession the immediate means for death —pills, poison, a rope, a gun, a car, access to heights, knives or razor.

DAY II   GOALS AND MEANS

GOAL   to recognize that dealing with a depressed or suicidal friend is scary but that taking a friend's feelings seriously as well as listening nonjudgmentally can be very helpful

MEANS   by participating in and responding to the moderately suicidal role play MICHAEL

GOAL   to explore the value of "reaching out to someone" rather than "holding it all inside"

MEANS   by exploring and discussing to whom adolescents might reach out

DAY II

What Can a Friend Do if He or She Begins to Pick Up on Suicidal Signs and Clues?

First of all, this can feel very threatening. "What if I say the wrong thing?" Naturally, it's scary and some people will feel like turning it off with something light like "Oh, come on, don't be silly!" or "Suicide is a dumb thing to do!" Another possibility is to back off and ignore warning signs, pretending that what one is sensing really can't be happening.

That is why help and support for the rescuer are so important. Suicide Prevention hotlines and professional therapists are sources where rescuers can check out with a trained counselor 1) whether the behavior and clues they are picking up on with a friend or relative sound suicidal or not; 2) directions and ideas on how to talk with this depressed or suicidal friend; 3) support for the rescuer's own fears of "blowing it" or his/her own feelings of helplessness in this situation. Bringing into the situation friends and adults whom one trusts also can disperse some of the sense of responsibility one may be experiencing as well as increase the support network for the friend who is feeling suicidal; 4) a plan for intervention if the individual is assessed as highly suicidal and a self-destructive act seems imminent.

While mental health professionals vary somewhat in their responses, there is a growing tendency not to hospitalize suicidal adolescents unless the individual is out of control and needs constant supervision in order to preserve life. In some instances an adolescent may choose to stay for a while in a mental hospital. A hospital can represent a secure place until the young person feels more in control of his/her life.

Students might want to check out the policies and norms of their own community in dealing with suicidal individuals.

If One Is Picking Up Suicidal Clues, Should a Person Talk about What He/She Is Suspecting with His/Her Friend? Is it Wrong to Ask "Are you Thinking of Killing Yourself?"

To help answer this question use MICHAEL ROLE-PLAY with class participants (see p. 117). When using the written script it is suggested that a student play the counselor and a teacher play the student. This role reversal puts the student in the role he or she may be asked to play in a real crisis. For dramatic impact, the teacher may be able to be more expressive in the dramatization. (Making two copies of this role play so that each participant has a copy in hand allows for greater flexibility.)

Suggest to students that as they listen to the role play they try to identify what Michael is feeling, the causes, and any suicidal clues that Michael may express. Ask students to be aware of how the counselor talks to Michael and what particular things the counselor says that seem to help Michael feel better.

Discussion after Michael Role Play

NOTE TO FACILITATOR:
The goal of discussion after the role play is to see 1) whether students have been able to pick up on signs of depression and sui-

cidal clues; 2) whether students have noticed the ways in which the counselor was able to reach out to the student.

Suggested questions that could be asked to move this discussion might be the following:

Was Michael suicidal? Where in the role play did you begin to suspect that Michael might be considering killing himself? What did he say that made you suspect that he might be suicidal?

What had been happening to Michael recently that had caused him to consider suicide? What kind of pain was he carrying? What had changed in his family as a result of his parent's divorce?

What seemed to help Michael feel better? What did the counselor do or say that seemed to help?

Was it okay for the counselor to come right out and ask Michael whether he was thinking of killing himself?

How does the role play end? What new courses of action did the counselor and Michael think might be alternatives to taking pills?

Other Types of Questions Facilitator Can Ask by Making Use of Role Play Quotes

What kinds of things did Michael say and what do you think Michael meant when he said . . . ?

"I just don't care anymore."

"I'm ready to hang it up."

"Nothing is going to change."

The level of desperation and sense of being trapped are strong clues that the student might be feeling suicidal. How the student copes with these feelings is crucial. There is a natural tendency to look for an escape from the pain. If the adolescent's life experience has not prepared him/her to cope with pain in constructive ways, he or she may see running away, drugs, alcohol, delinquency, pregnancy, or suicide as escape routes.

"Yesterday was the last straw."

The despair voiced by Michael in this role play was triggered by an event that felt like the last straw—one where the individual suddenly finds the pain too much to bear. Unable to endure it any longer, the person may feel crazy enough, desperate enough to try something impulsively self-destructive. To an outsider, a desperate response to a last-straw event may seem out of proportion. It is important to realize that it is usually not an isolated event. It is magnified for the individual because it is the latest in a series of rejections or losses. That is why it is important for a friend or counselor to find out what else has been happening in the individual's life.

"They [parents] just yelled at me! How stupid I am and irresponsible!"

Lack of trust or appreciation from other family members can foster feelings of worthlessness in a person. Such feelings are deepened when friends, too, don't seem to care enough to listen. The result may be an increasing sense of being cut off from everyone, spiraling downward into a heavier sense of worthlessness.

"I've got some pills. . . I might as well. I'm no good at anything."

When a person is in possession of the means for taking his/her own life, it is essential to talk through with the person other alternatives to suicide, ways to cope with suffering other than suicide, possible ways to change the unbearable situation. At the same time it is important both to find some way of removing the means, such as getting rid of pills, and also to make sure a seriously suicidal person is *not left alone*.

Was It Okay to Ask Michael if He Was Feeling Suicidal?

Contrary to the popular myth that to talk openly about suicide will encourage a person to try it, it can be very beneficial to ask a person if he or she is thinking about suicide. Usually there is a real sense of relief in being able to talk about suicidal feelings. It relieves the tension of keeping such a burden secret. Also, once such feelings are out in the open, the young person may be able to accept the kind of help and support he or she needs in order to change the situation.

What Seemed to Help Michael Feel Better?
What Did the Counselor Do or Say?

Just talking about what one is feeling releases a lot of pain. It is not all held inside any more. To be able to have someone really listen, to experience real acceptance of what one is feeling can make one feel less alone. A nonjudgmental listener allows the despairing young person to release pain as well as to legitimize as valid what he or she is experiencing. "No wonder you feel so bummed out. No wonder you hurt."

While listening and empathy don't change the basic situation, it can help a young person feel somewhat less desperate to realize that he or she has reasons others can respect for feeling this bad. It can help adolescents to feel more lovable, to trust him or her self more, to feel some renewed sense of hope.

One of the characteristics of suicidal people is a kind of tunnel vision. They are standing so close to their problems that they can't seem to see any other way out. Besides being a nonjudgmental listener and helping the friend tell his/her experience, a counselor/friend can help the suicidal person get some perspective by exploring other ways out. "Have you ever considered trying . . . ? Do you think if you tried . . . ?"

How Does the Role Play End? What New Courses
of Action Did the Counselor and Student Think Might
Be Alternatives to Taking the Pills?

Usually suicidal feelings develop from feeling like a failure or feeling cut off from those one loves. In the Michael role play, the possibility of Michael's re-establishing contact with the aunt and maybe some communication with the real mother represented new options. It broadened his perspective. Contacting both of these people might also expand Michael's support system. When one is feeling as much pain as the adolescent in the role play, one needs as much support as one can get.

Who Are Some of the People an Adolescent in Pain Might Reach Out to? How Might These People Be Helpful?

NOTE TO FACILITATOR:

Using the blackboard, facilitator can elicit not only possibili-ties but also the pros and cons of reaching out to any of the sug-gested individuals. Facilitator can suggest to students that on their own time they might want to think about which individuals in their own lives they might trust enough to share depressed or suicidal feelings with.

friends

a trusted teacher, coach, guidance counselor

neighbors

parents of friends

minister, rabbi, priest

professional counseling help

relatives

school drop-in program

suicide prevention or crisis hotline

Parents or brothers and sisters may be at the core of the ad-olescent's pain. While one might like to reach out to these indi-viduals the most, they may be the hardest ones to talk with at first. Talking with trusted friends or other less involved adults may be where to start. However, the important thing is to *reach out*. There are no gold stars for facing crises and pain all alone. We're all human. We all need support, sometimes desperately. It is not a failure to need help. It is sensible to recognize when one needs special help and to reach out to those who can give us what we need. Life is too precious to throw away because of a temporary sense of despair.

DAY III GOALS AND MEANS

GOAL to help students become more aware of the fact that alleviating depression involves taking more control over their own lives

MEANS by creating a dialogue based on broad questions such as:

How can one get rid of depression?
How can one change one's personal situation?
What stops an adolescent from taking more control over his/her life?

by helping students to recognize that taking control is hard to do and involves facing fear plus the problem of dealing with one's anger

GOAL to help students begin to think about such questions as:

What keeps me alive?
What do I live for?
What do I need to change in order to live better?

MEANS by discussing questions and by providing students with time for writing down their own personal answers to the above questions

Senior High School

DAY III

How Does One Cope with Depression?

NOTE TO FACILITATOR:
Effectiveness of this discussion, which is most helpful when personalized, largely depends on the trust levels that have been built up in the classroom between students and the facilitator. While making oneself overly vulnerable through exposure of one's feelings would not be appropriate, some mutual sharing from students who are depressed or have worked through those feelings can create an invaluable atmosphere for others who feel "very alone." Focus needs to be placed on the fact that being depressed or feeling pain at certain times in our lives is a normal human condition. Many adolescents assume they are the only ones who have ever felt this way.

A nonthreatening beginning for this discussion is to start with Useful Personal Coping Strategies *found in the Jr. High Program, pages 109 to 110. In a natural way students will want to move this discussion beyond temporary coping solutions toward a more in depth approach to solving the sources of their depression.*

How Can One Get Rid of Depression?

Being depressed is triggered by loss or rejection. It is an anger turned inward because of one's powerlessness to heal the hurt.

Getting rid of depression involves figuring out where it is coming from. Sometimes an adolescent is aware of a number of things that are wrong but hasn't pieced together that all of them together are feeding into a real sense of despair. It can be helpful to remind students of "Karen's Mountain," discussed on the first day of the program. Karen's mountain grew out of layers of problems.

Once an adolescent (or anyone for that matter) has pinpointed what is causing it, lifting the depression involves making changes in one's thinking or one's life situation or both. It necessitates taking more control over one's life. It also requires an act of will to say to one's self "I'm not going to put up with this any longer! I want to wake up in the morning feeling good about the day! What do I have to do to change and what do I want changed in my life situation?" It means asking a very important question of one's self. "What do I want or need *now* in order to live more fully?" and "How can I get what I need?"

How Can One Change One's Personal Situation? Isn't that Hard to Do?

Change is always difficult. Taking more responsibility for one's life and thereby increasing control over and respect for our personhood and position at home, at school, and in the community can be a scary endeavor.

While environmental change may be the most critical change needed, it can also have an inflexible component. It is easy to become discouraged, and thereby fall back into angry depression. In such cases, the young person may need outside help in learning more adaptive ways to cope with the situation so that some personal sense of control over the environment (most often the home situation) is possible.

However, usually any environmental change requires some

behavioral changes or different ways of handling problem situations. Sometimes young people look on changing a personal behavior pattern as an insidious adult tactic to increase adult control. Young people fear an increase in their already acute sense of powerlessness.

While it is true that adolescents have very little material power, dependent as they are on the family for food and shelter, and the school for education, adolescents can find ways to meet their emotional needs.

Much of this falls back on becoming clear in one's own head on *what* is needed and then going about learning how to get it.

What Stops Adolescents from Changing/ From Taking More Control Over Their Lives?

Fear

> Fear of being alone
>
> Fear of being rejected if one reaches out for one's own needs
>
> Fear of being independent in a world that feels very hostile
>
> Fear of being physically abused

Such fears are very real and in some cases a tragic possibility. This makes the stakes pretty high when one is thinking about seeking more control. These fears have powerful overtones, particularly if the family situation includes any of the following: spouse or child abuse, alcoholism, or unemployment. Sometimes all four of these problems go together. Without denying the reality of these fears, it is important to underscore the fact with young people that in addition to outside adults who might be supportive, there are agencies and laws which can serve in an advocacy role for an adolescent.

The fear of being alone is probably the most poignant fear. While the need for love and caring from others is a basic human need, at some abstract level everyone is alone. Nobody else can be born for us or do our living. Our feelings and our actions are ours, even though at times we may feel like puppets on a string.

Embracing independence is a frightening but also very liberating proposition. It leads to being responsible for who we are. If we want to be responsible, then we must know who we are, and this involves constant awareness of our needs, our wants, limits, and feelings. It also requires scrupulous honesty and considerable courage. The pay-off is that we can be in the driver's seat with control over the direction in which we're going.

Anger

Anger often creates fear because it so often leads to a feeling of being out of control. We may be afraid to express anger because it may make us vulnerable to retaliation from some one more powerful than we are. Or we may be afraid of hurting someone we love. Often we turn this anger in upon ourselves, substituting a holding pattern (depression) instead of confronting and/or seeking resolutions to the problem.

No two people are likely to see things exactly alike, so conflict is a natural consequence of the differences between people. Conflicts are resolved either through suppression (depression), force, or negotiation. The consequences of suppression can lead to depression which we are trying to avoid. Force usually leads to resentment (maybe more depression) but often to revenge. Negotiation may involve giving up something on both sides, but, if done in a spirit of respect, can lead to a feeling on both sides that both have won something valuable. This form of negotiation, known as win-win, is useful for parents and adolescents to learn because it deals with power issues in such a way as to make the parties to conflict allies rather than adversaries.

Inappropriate Expectations

Life is difficult for everyone; however, everyone has a right to a quality of living that provides a good life. Many people (and particularly adolescents) interpret this to mean that they are obliged to be happy, and if they aren't happy all of the time (i.e. if they suffer pain), something outside themselves (the family, the school, the government) is violating this right and needs fixing; or that there is something wrong with themselves and *they* need fixing. Narrowly seeing problems as only coming from "out there," or conversely, blaming one's self as being somehow inadequate in the world, leads to feelings of helplessness and worthlessness, as if one is a reject from a system that everyone else seems to be able to function in.

Living fully is an ongoing process of growing and changing to meet the "out-there" problems that confront and confuse our internal life.

Is It Helpful to Develop a Personal Philosophy of Life?

NOTE TO FACILITATOR:
In order to bring this global concept of developing a "philosophy of life" into more manageable focus, the following questions can be asked:

What keeps me alive?
What do I live for? What do I find myself looking forward to?
What do I need to change in order to live better?

After discussion of these questions, adolescents might benefit from having some time in class to write down their own responses to these questions, not to hand in but to keep for their own personal enrichment or to share with others with whom they feel close.

Junior or Senior High School

DAY IV   GOALS AND MEANS

OPTIONAL DAY

GOAL   to try out and develop some listening awareness skills to use when talking with a depressed and/or suicidal friend

MEANS   by creating spontaneous role play situations using unconnected telephones

GOAL   to get honest evaluation (feedback) from students as to the personal value of The *Living* Alternative Program Unit

MEANS   by filling out an evaluation sheet anonymously

(optional) by providing the option for giving one's name if student desires some personal follow-up on a one-to-one basis may be possible. If no resources are available in the school and student gives permission, names of such students could be passed on to a community crisis-oriented agency for telephone or face-to-face follow-up.

by taking a content test (without grades) in order to evaluate what a student has learned from the program. (Test is only appropriate for Senior High.)

Junior or Senior High School

DAY IV

Role Plays of Crisis Counseling Situations Using Unconnected Telephones

NOTE TO FACILITATOR:
Persons in crisis no longer feel they can cope with the situation. They may be feeling quite desperate. Finding oneself as the counselor/friend confronted by such a person can be alarming. One highly useful enrichment to the Living Alternatives Program is role-playing some counseling calls and thereby getting some practice either through participation or modeling.

While an adolescent can learn a great deal from role playing and the activity can be fun, initially it may be somewhat difficult to muster enthusiasm. Fear of making a fool of one's self or embarrassment at revealing one's own problems in front of peers is justifiably threatening. Using real telephones and having the call supposedly coming to a Crisis Service can provide a degree of security and distance. The telephone company is generally quite willing to lend telephones from their business office for educational purposes. Using real telephones and not "play phones" is essential if facilitator wants to impart an aura of seriousness to the role plays.

The following counseling suggestions can be put on a blackboard to give adolescents direction in how to listen to an adolescent who calls in crisis:

1. Try to be nonjudgmental and just listen.
2. Ask open-ended questions that allow the caller to talk as fully as possible about what he or she is feeling and what the young person is experiencing.

> "Tell me about what happened?"
> "How did that make you feel?"
> "Has this happened other times? How was this time similar to/ different from before?"

3. Be supportive if possible.

> "That sounds awful."
> "No wonder you're angry/hurt."

4. Instead of giving direct advice . . .

> "Have you thought about doing . . . ?"
> "What do you think would happen if you tried . . . ?"

Encourage counselor/student to respond to the person who calls in ways one would like oneself if he or she happened to be the person in crisis.

Coming up with possible role plays can be a stumbling block. If students do not come with possible role plays on their own, suggest that the student who is pretending to be the counselor from a hotline service leave the room while teacher and other students come up with problems a student could be calling a hotline about. Encourage students to create problems and crisis situations that an adolescent might truly experience. The real value of these role plays is lost if the student caller can't get into the role play because the situation is too far removed from anything a young person could have experienced.

If the locality does have a local hotline, use their phone number for dialing. Since the phones are disconnected, another student needs to make a ringing sound to cue counselor into picking up the phone. Students become involved in all of these logistics and this usually helps to dispel anxiety about peer reaction. Even discussion about how to answer the call is useful. Will counselor answer the ring with "Hello" or with something like "Crisis Hotline. Can I help you?"

Allow the call to go on for only a few minutes unless it is going extremely well. Chances are that the adolescent counselor will get bogged down, flounder for words, begin to feel helpless, and start giving *lots of advice*, or else begin to mouth "What do I do now?" If the facilitator begins to sense any of this, stop the role play call and begin to process what was going on in the call as a way of helping adolescents understand what they were feeling and what they were saying. If the participants are embarrassed, one can support them by saying that no one expects them to be experts. This is a learning experience and it is far better to flounder in a role play than in a real situation.

In order to process what was going on in the role play call and help the group gain some insight into "how to listen," questions to the caller and to the listener might be as follows:

Questions that could be asked of the adolescent caller:

1. How did you feel about the call?
2. Was the counselor helpful?
3. What did he or she say that made you feel better?
4. What did you want the counselor to say but he or she didn't?

Questions that could be asked of the adolescent counselor:

1. How did you feel about the call?
2. What were you trying to do in the call?

3. Was there any place where you wanted to say something but didn't? What held you back? What were you afraid would happen if you said what you wanted to say?
4. Was there any place where you didn't know what to say? What do you think it was that threw you? Can you think what you'd say another time?

Talk over with students the problem most individuals have when someone they know is hurting—the desire to rescue them, make them feel better—immediately. We may not be able to do that.

In fact, we can't solve someone else's problems, but it can be extremely valuable to have someone listen, to find someone who will somehow make it all right to really talk about what one is feeling. The value is that the friend is no longer carrying his or her pain and anger totally alone. Someone else knows. That can be a real release for the friend as well as helping the adolescent feel less isolated. If this friend also can get some perspective on what he or she is feeling, the adolescent may come up with an alternative, a course of action that is worth trying. Just talking about one's problems out loud can sometimes substantially clarify what one needs to do.

These kinds of listening skills are usually new to adolescents. By going through a number of role plays with comparable time for feedback, young people may be able to pick up some invaluable information on ways to reach out (what they ought to expect from talking to someone) and how to listen to a friend (what they can do and what they won't be able to do).

Evaluation of the *Living* Alternative Program

Student Evaluation

The *Living* Alternative Program evaluation by students can be extremely helpful.

1. It underscores the serious intent of the program to impart information about important life skills.

2. It supports listening and nonjudgmental acceptance of an adolescent's evaluation and opinions.
3. It provides an opportunity for a young person to initiate further discussion by putting his/her name at the bottom of the evaluation sheet. The responder can be a teacher, crisis worker, or other, but adolescents need to know in advance (if they sign their name) who will call. It provides an opportunity to pick up on students who may be dealing with crisis/suicide/depression but have been unable to verbalize their needs in a larger group.
4. It allows the facilitator to get useful feedback on what worked or didn't work in the presentation of the material. There is an opportunity for some self-assessment.

Teacher Evaluation

If the facilitator for the program comes from outside the school system, such as from a crisis service or mental health agency, the teacher evaluation can be additionally helpful in assessment of the content absorption and/or attitude about the presentation of the facilitator.

SUICIDE PREVENTION EDUCATIONAL PROGRAM

Student Evaluation

Dates of Program _____

School _____

1. We have spent time talking about what it feels like to be depressed or in painful situations. We talked about feeling trapped or rejected, and what to do if you or someone you know is feeling suicidal. In what ways do you feel these discussions have been helpful?

2. If there were parts of this program that were not especially helpful, could you indicate what they were and why they weren't helpful?

3. Are there other things that you would like to see included in this program?

4. If you would like to talk further, jot down your name, phone number, and best time to reach you.

Name _____

Phone _____

Best Time to Call _____

SUICIDE PREVENTION EDUCATIONAL PROGRAM

Teacher Evaluation

Dates of Program ———————————————————————————

School ————————————————————————————————————

Teacher ————————————————————————————————————

1. What do you feel your students gained from this program?

2. Were there issues that were not presented that you would like to see included?

3. How would you evaluate the way the program was presented?

4. Other comments

Testing for Content Presentation

Attaching grades to this unit on suicide and depression is probably counterproductive. The goals of the *Living* Alternative Program underscore the fact that knowledge and self-awareness of the dynamics of depression and suicide are essential life skills.

However, in order for both teachers and students to evaluate whether these life skills have been absorbed, it can be useful to give a test such as the one that follows after this unit is presented. High scores and answers to essay-type questions will provide both teachers and students with a realistic assessment as to whether the program material was truly transferred into cognitive learning.

DEPRESSION/SUICIDE/CRISIS   Name＿＿＿＿＿＿Period＿＿

1. Identify two common myths surrounding the issue of suicide.

   a.

   b.

2. Choose one of the above myths and explain why it is false.

3. What does length of time and the intensity of depression have to do with a depressed person becoming suicidal?

4. List two indications or signs of depression.

   a.

   b.

5. List three suicidal clues/warning signals a person might give if he/she was thinking about committing suicide.

   a.

   b.

   c.

6. What are two ways a person might try to help a suicidal friend?

7. Which of the following causes for suicide is the most common?
   a) loneliness   b) depression   c) revenge
   d) manipulation of others

8. Which of the following would *not* indicate that a person is thinking of committing suicide?
   a) A person talking or writing about suicide.
   b) A person making final arrangements and giving away personal possessions.
   c) A person whose mother is in a mental institution.
   d) Change in personality or behavior of a person.

9. Which of the following is *true* about suicide?
   a) Suicide usually happens with warning signals.
   b) Suicide only occurs in a specific class of people.
   c) Suicidal tendencies are inherited.
   d) Only professionals can help a suicidal person.

10. Which of the following statements is *not true* about suicide?
   a) A person who talks about suicide is thinking about suicide.
   b) It is estimated that 5,000 adolescents succeed in killing themselves every year.
   c) Only psychiatrists can prevent a person from committing suicide.

11. Which of the following may accompany depression:
   a) Loss of appetite.
   b) Withdrawal from friends and from relatives.
   c) Loss of sleep or excessive sleep accompanied by fatigue.

    d) Difficulty in ability to concentrate.
    e) All of the above.

12. Which of the following statements is *true* about suicide?
    a) Only mentally ill people commit suicide.
    b) Suicidal tendencies are passed on through the genes.
    c) Wanting to commit suicide usually reflects a temporary state of despair.
    d) People who say they are going to commit suicide really won't do it.

DAY V   GOALS AND MEANS

OPTIONAL DAY

GOAL   to give students additional confidence and knowledge that working through depression and/or suicidal feelings is possible

MEANS   by bringing a guest into the classroom who has been suicidal to talk from his/her own personal experience in learning skills for living

GOAL   to answer content questions about suicide where students may have specific concerns and/or anxiety

MEANS   by bringing into the classroom a crisis hotline worker and/or mental health professional who has had experience working with depressed or suicidal persons

GOAL   to explore some of the community resources where an adolescent could reach out for help with personal or family problems

MEANS   discussion and use of "Crisis Cards" if these are available (See pages 145-147)

Junior or Senior High School

DAY V

Guest Speaker/s

For adolescents it is very powerful on the final day of the program to bring into the classroom a guest speaker who has previously been suicidal and has been able to work through those feelings. The speaker lends a certain credibility to what the students have been learning. Also, to be face to face with someone who has dealt with suicidal feelings and come out on the other side represents hope.

Another speaker option is to bring in someone from a local crisis hotline service who would be able to answer questions about available community services. This person could also answer *Content Questions About Suicide Most Frequently Asked by Adolescents*. (See next page)

Frequently, it may be possible to have an outside speaker who can cover both of these areas such as a person who has been suicidal but who now works for a crisis hotline service.

In some cases, the facilitator for the *Living* Alternatives Program may be from the outside: such as a crisis hotline service or a community mental health facility. Classroom teachers and/or group leaders have the outside speaker option if it is appropriate to their particular situation.

Content Questions about Suicide
Most Frequently Asked by Adolescents

The content questions and answers about suicide on the succeeding pages can be used in conjunction with a visit from a guest speaker on the last day of the program. They also could be used as a program option anywhere in the program. There may be occasions, such as a last-minute substitution of a new facilitator or a student group finding difficulty getting into a discussion, when it would be useful to have a prescribed list of questions about suicide. The use of these questions and answers could help a substitute facilitator avert his or her own feelings of panic in re "What do I do now?"

With copies of the questions for everyone, students can choose to ask the questions that most concern them. While brief answers to these questions are included in this section, fuller answers to some questions are to be found in the content of the Junior and Senior High Program material.

Some of the content covered in the answers to these questions is not covered in the program materials due to its specificity; however, it is advisable for a facilitator to be prepared to answer these questions since some adolescents may spontaneously raise them during the course of the program.

Questions about Suicide

1. Why do people commit suicide?
2. What are the main reasons that teenagers commit suicide?
3. Is it true that people attempt suicide as a cry for help?
4. If someone in the family has committed suicide, may others in the family be tempted to commit suicide when they have problems.?
5. Do people ever attempt suicide to get attention or to get others to feel sorry for them?

6. If a person attempts suicide and fails, what is the likelihood of the attempter trying again?
7. Is it true that people who attempt to kill themselves really don't want to die?
8. Will a person who is deeply depressed always become suicidal?
9. Does anyone ever impulsively try to kill him or her self and then become sorry for making such an attempt?
10. Does taking drugs or alcohol increase one's chances of becoming suicidal?
11. How can one help a person who is suicidal?
12. How does talking about suicide help prevent it?
13. Is suicide or attempted suicide against the law?
14. Is a person who attempts suicide mentally ill?
15. Can suicidal people be put into a mental institution against their will?
16. What effects does a suicide have on the individual's remaining family and relatives?
17. Why do some people keep secret that there has been a suicide in the family?
18. What are the most common methods for teenagers to commit suicide?
19. Is there a particular hour of the day that is the most common time for attempting suicide?
20. Is there any particular group or class of people who are more likely to become suicidal?
21. How many teenagers each year actually succeed in killing themselves?

    How many more make attempts on their lives?
    How many seriously contemplate suicide?
22. Do more men or women make attempts on their lives?
23. Does everybody think about committing suicide at least once in their lifetime?

Answers to Questions about Suicide

1. People who commit suicide are having intense feelings of helplessness and hopelessness, and don't see any other way out. Revenge may also be a motive.

2. Teenagers who commit suicide are feeling unloved/rejected or perceive themselves as failures in their families or in relationships.

3. The suicide attempt is often a conscious or unconscious method for getting others to recognize just how badly the individual is feeling.

4. If someone in the family has committed suicide, other family members may be more tempted because that behavior has been modeled for them; however, there is not a genetic disposition for suicide.

5. Anyone who attempts suicide in order to get attention desperately needs attention. It is tragic when young people feel they need to bargain with their life in order to have their problems taken seriously.

6. More than 50 percent of those who complete suicide have made a prior suicide attempt; however, many people who receive concerned help after a suicide attempt never become suicidal again.

7. Most people who kill themselves are ambivalent about whether to live or die right up to the moment of death.

8. While it is true that suicidal feelings most often develop in a person who is deeply depressed, the fact that one is depressed does not mean that a person will become suicidal.

9. A person at a particular moment may find the emotional pain they are experiencing absolutely intolerable. In that short period they might impulsively make a suicide attempt which in retrospect they regret having done.

10. Taking drugs and alcohol in excess can exaggerate painful feelings to a point where they are intolerable. In that state a person who otherwise would not go that far might attempt suicide.

11. A person who is feeling that life is too painful to continue being a part of usually believes him or herself to be very worthless and unloved. Showing such individuals some real caring by listening to and accepting their feelings, staying close and getting others to be supportive can really help them feel that it's worth going on after all.

12. Talking about suicide diffuses some of the intensity of these

feelings. It helps the person get connected to the help that is needed. It creates a climate of caring and helps to break through the loneliness the person is experiencing.

13. Suicide or attempted suicide used to be against the law. In some states, it is only within the last decade that suicide has ceased to be a crime. It is still illegal to assist someone in committing suicide, as in euthanasia.

14. The majority of people who attempt suicide are not mentally ill, but are individuals who are feeling that their lives are intolerable. With a kind of tunnel vision they are unable to see any other way out except suicide.

15. A suicidal person can be involuntarily committed for 48 hours or 72 hours (NY State law) if the individual is out of control and/or there is a psychological assessment that the individual would take his/her life if left alone. This is an extreme measure used for the preservation of life.

16. "The suicide leaves his psychological skeleton in the emotional closet of his survivors" (Edwin Schneidman, University of California). The survivors of a suicide are left to struggle with complex feelings of rage, guilt, despair, grief, and shame. Recovery from the loss of a loved one by suicide is the hardest form of grief to resolve.

17. Some people keep secret the fact that there has been a suicide in the family out of fear of being blamed and socially ostracized. While this has been true in the past, fortunately much of the stigma is lifting and people are dealing with suicide more directly and honestly.

18. Lethal methods used for attempting suicide by teenagers are hanging, guns, jumping, carbon monoxide poisoning, and drug overdoses. Car accidents account for many deaths, but it is often difficult to determine whether the death is suicide or an accident.

19. Young people, who are probably the most ambivalent suicides, tend to make attempts in the morning or around dinnertime when there is likelihood of rescue.

20. Suicide is as prevalent in professional families as in working class families; however, in this country there have been proportionally more whites than blacks taking their own lives.

21. According to statistics compiled by the National Institute for Mental Health:

    5,000 teenagers each year succeed in killing themselves.

    50,000–100,000 teenagers make attempts on their lives.

    As many as 200,000–300,000 may contemplate suicide. Since many possible suicides and attempted suicides are listed as accidents, the numbers probably are much higher.

22. Although many more women than men make attempts on their lives, more men actually succeed in killing themselves. This is due to the fact that men who try usually use more lethal methods such as guns. Women are more likely to use pills.

23. Most people will have fleeting thoughts of suicide at some point in their lives.

PART II
Junior High School
FOUR-DAY LIVING ALTERNATIVES PROGRAM

Junior High School

DAY I   GOALS AND MEANS

GOAL   to establish trust between facilitator and students and to facilitate the creation of a climate where students can feel comfortable about giving honest answers to questions

MEANS   by creating an atmosphere of informality and seriousness, listening to student responses nonjudgmentally

by being supportive of student attempts to deal with questions out of their own experience

GOAL   to talk about suicide and depression, both what they represent and the causes

MEANS   by discussion and listening to the Karen role play

Junior High School

DAY I

Why Talk about Suicide?

Unfortunately, it has become very important to talk about suicide because more and more young people are taking their own lives. In the last 20 years the rate of suicides among teenagers has increased 300 percent. Suicide is not just something that happens elsewhere; it is happening right in our own locality. Nationally, adolescent suicide has risen to the point where it has become the number three cause of death, with car accidents being number one.

As with most adverse events, the more we know, the better able we are to understand and therefore prevent. If we can learn to recognize the signs of suicidal behavior, understand the reasons for feeling suicidal, and what to do in such an emergency, we may truly be able to help avert a tragedy.

Why Would Anyone Want To Commit Suicide, Particularly a Teenager?

People who are thinking about killing themselves are individuals who are trying to get away from feeling unbearable pain. They feel helpless to change things. They are hopeless and despairing of their lives ever getting any better. It is not that they want to die, they just can't think of any other way to stop the pain.

What Are Some of the Things that Could Cause a Person to Feel Really Unhappy? What Could Happen at School or at Home that Might Be Really Hard to Deal with?

1) Being picked on at school.
2) Feeling that one doesn't have any close friends.
3) Feeling like a failure.
4) Feeling that one isn't good at anything.
5) Being unhappy at home because of divorce or family conflict. Feeling rejected by one or both parents. Or feeling a conflict of loyalties ("Which parent shall I live with?") Maybe feeling guilty ("This divorce, or these problems in the family, might not be happening if I could be a better son or daughter.") Putting oneself down ("It's probably all my fault. There must be something wrong with me.")
6) Distress due to chronic family problems that seem to require secrecy such as physical or sexual abuse or alcoholism. These can stir in a young person continuing confusion, pain, and shame.
7) Any kind of loss—loss of a best friend or close relative either through death or moving away ("How can I get along without this person in my life? Now there's nobody to share things with.")

Not everyone will react in the same way to painful situations. Some young people are more sensitive to pain than others. It doesn't mean that these adolescents are weaker or somehow less capable than others; it simply means that, for whatever reasons, some tough situations are just harder to cope with than others for some people at certain times in their lives.

Adolescents usually don't have that backlog of experience

to realize that pain really does soften with time. They tend to expect it to disappear quickly. In fact, this is certainly what TV and modern society has modeled. If you have a Pepsi or take a pill, everything looks brighter. Pain is rough and there are no magical cures, but there are ways to cope with pain. There are ways to feel better other than running away from home, or getting high on drugs, or bombing into oblivion with alcohol, or driving a car at 95 mph, or wandering through day after day in total gloom; certainly other than slashing wrists, or taking pills.

How Does One Cope with Pain?
Does It Help to Tell Someone?

One very important way to cope with pain is to reach out to someone who will listen. Sometimes that is hard to do. We can get locked in, feeling no one cares. So we may reason, "Why would anyone want to listen to me?" Therefore it is also important, if one senses that a friend is depressed, to reach out in some way, in the hope of helping the friend to feel a little less alone, to make it a little easier to talk about what it is that's so upsetting. "Hey, you've seemed really down lately, can I listen? Is there anything I can do?"

Act out the Role Play Script (p. 122)

NOTE TO FACILITATOR:
Suggest to students that as they watch the role play they try to figure out what Karen is feeling and why. Elicit from students whether they think Karen is suicidal or not and what Karen says that supports their perceptions. After the role play, ask the above questions again. In order to further guide discussion, the facilitator might pick up on student responses to Karen's feelings by asking . . .

What Do You Think Karen Was Feeling When She Said ". . .It's Like I'm Falling into a Hole and I Don't Know Where I Am or Who I Am."

Karen was feeling very confused about herself, so confused that it was like groping around in a dark hole. That's a pretty scary feeling. "I feel like I'm blending into the walls of the school . . . I'm the ugliest brick in the school . . ."

Karen felt ugly. She felt quite worthless and very lonely. There was much hopelessness expressed when she thought about herself as just a faceless brick blending into a faceless wall.

"I just felt so worthless. I felt so alone."

Karen had had a very painful experience at school. The high school had a tradition where on Valentine's Day, students gave each of their friends a single carnation. Students wore these flowers all day long. Karen did not receive a single flower. It was a last straw for her. Often it is a painful "last straw event" that prompts a person, who is already feeling trapped and worthless, to consider suicide seriously.

Was Karen Suicidal or Not?

Karen said . . . "Weekends are okay. After school is okay . . ."

Karen still had places in her life where she felt okay. It was only when she was in school that she felt left out and worthless. For people who are suicidal, it often seems as if every door in their lives is being shut in their face. They see no way out.

Also, Karen was reaching out for help. She wasn't totally cut off and hopeless. She was feeling much pain, but she wanted things to get better and was trying to get help.

Talking with someone doesn't solve the problems, but it can provide relief and cast a ray of light. A person feels less alone. For Karen the pain isn't all locked up inside any more. It's out in the open where she can look at it and get some ideas on how to deal with the situation.

The probability is that Karen isn't suicidal. She does appear to be anxious and depressed.

Do Depression and Suicide Go Together?
Is a Person Who Is Depressed Going to
Become Suicidal?

While it is true that people who have been depressed for a long time may become suicidal—because they don't want to hurt anymore—because they can't stand feeling depressed any-more—being depressed doesn't necessarily mean that one is going to become suicidal.

Everyone has times when they are depressed. Sometimes a person feels bummed out for a few hours or a few weeks. But if depression goes on and on or seems to get more and more "depressing," it is important to get some help and figure out what is going on. There are usually reasons for a person staying depressed day after day after day.

Even in that event, being severely depressed doesn't mean a person is going to become suicidal.

DAY II   GOALS AND MEANS

GOAL   to help students legitimize the feelings they may have about their own painful experiences

MEANS   by continuing the story of Karen, building a mountain of possible problems around her

by graphically showing how depressed and/or suicidal feelings can develop

GOAL   to explore with students where a young person might reach out if he or she needed help with problems

MEANS   by supporting the value of reaching out for help and by creating a list on the blackboard of possible "helping persons"

GOAL   to explore with students the concept of coping skills as methods of helping themselves get through painful times

MEANS   by talking about pets as coping mechanisms and by forming a long list on the blackboard of other possible things to do for oneself when feeling trapped, depressed, and lonely

Junior High School

DAY II

How Can Suicidal Feelings Develop?

NOTE TO FACILITATOR:
The phone call from Karen was very short. There is much about Karen's life that is still unknown. Using a blackboard, facilitator can help class create a story about Karen. By building layers of problems around Karen, class can begin to see how the burden of painful feelings and problems could lead to someone becoming suicidal.

1) Start with drawing an unhappy Karen stick figure.

2) What was Karen feeling?
These aren't pleasant feelings, but they are ones most people feel at least some of the time.

3) What could happen to Karen at home that might be hard for her to deal with, might cause her to become unhappy?
Divorce or loss of a parent are usually suggested by students, but any combination of painful possibilities can be used to build a mountain over Karen.

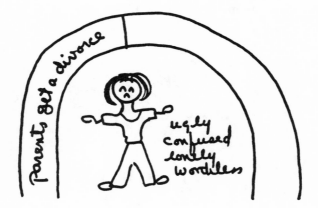

4) How might a divorce in the family make her feel?

    a) Guilty: Because maybe if she'd done this or that, her parents might have stayed together.

    b) Rejected: "Maybe I'm not very lovable because my dad (or mom) moved out."

    c) Conflicted: "Who should I live with? If I choose this one, will the other one be hurt? I don't want to hurt either of my parents."

    d) Angry: Because this happened it has become hard to talk about it with either parent.

    e) Lost and hurt: Just missing the way things were. Missing the parent one doesn't see as often.

5) How might this situation at home affect Karen at school? One usually carries what is happening at home to school. One can't just shut the door when one leaves home in the morning and leave one's feelings at home, too. Karen may be feeling pretty depressed.

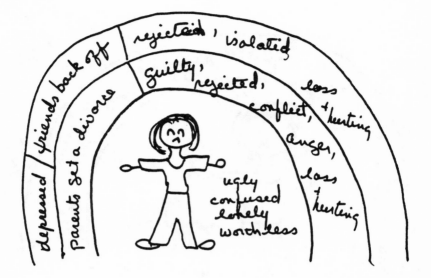

If Karen is depressed, is that likely to effect her relationships with other students or friends?

A person who is depressed is no fun to be around. Friends may back off and she may begin to feel rejection, loss, isolation at school, too, as well as at home. Now Karen may be feeling ugly, confused, lonely, worthless, rejected, lost at home and at school, and quite isolated from the people she cares about in both places. These could add up to a lot of negative painful feelings piling up over her.

6) Is this situation likely to affect her school work and grades?

It is extremely hard to study when one is terribly depressed. Sometimes it is almost physically impossible to study. When one is trying so hard not to think about what is troubling one, then it is terribly difficult to concentrate on anything.

And yet, many people don't understand this very real aspect of "being depressed." Teachers and/or parents can come down pretty hard on an adolescent for not studying. The adolescent may be told "to get it together" or "You're not being very responsible."

This increases the depression because the young person can begin to feel like a failure, to feel generally worthless.

The situation for Karen appears to be spiraling, with one problem getting stacked on another. If this is what has been happening to Karen, she also could begin to feel trapped, and unable to see a way out.

Let us suppose that the one thing Karen feels really good about is being on the swim team. Often, it is our hobbies or extracurricular activities that bring us the most joy. One goes in for these activities because one is good at them, or has gotten good at them through a lot of practice. Other people may admire us for our skill, form, or endurance. In this case being on the swim team is probably one aspect of Karen's life that feels positive.

If Karen is on the swim team as her "good place in the midst of so many negative things," what is likely to happen to Karen if she can't study?

Her grades may go down.

What is likely to happen to Karen's status on the team if her grades go down? She is likely to be kicked off the team. It may seem that that last door—to that last place where she feels good about herself—is now shut on her.

At this point could one conceive of the possibility of Karen becoming suicidal? What is there for her to live for? She might be saying "How can I get out of *this*?" "What use is it to try *anything* anymore?" "Everything is going wrong!" "I've lost everything that means anything to me."

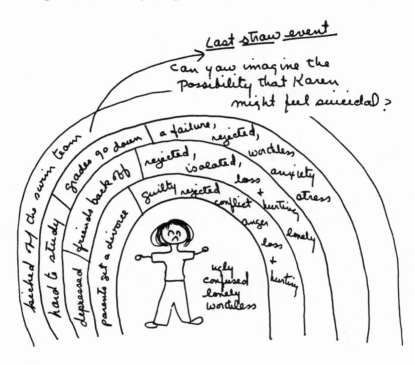

If Karen Becomes Suicidal as a Result of this "Mountain of Problems," What Can She Do? What Can You Do? Who Can She Reach Out to?

NOTE TO FACILITATOR:

Use of a blackboard can be helpful so that young people can see graphically that there are a number of possibilities when one is having problems. It also supports not trying to handle everything alone.

a trusted friend

a teacher one feels comfortable with

neighbor

coach

minister, rabbi, priest

parents of friends

other relatives

a professional counselor or therapist, local helping agencies

brothers or sisters

parents

Reaching out can help! It does relieve the experience of feeling so alone, so weighted down that the layers can feel overwhelming.

But What if Karen Doesn't Reach Out?

One of the characteristics of suicidal people is feeling so worthless that they wonder "Why would anyone care?" It is important to remember that suicidal people don't want to die; they just want the pain to stop. They may be able to tell a best friend what they are feeling but then they may try to swear that friend to secrecy. "Don't tell anyone!"

If You Are that Friend, What Do You Do?

Obviously, you tell someone and get help for Karen. Yes, one's friend might be angry, but this friend probably wouldn't tell you about these feelings if he or she really wanted to die. The chances are that with help from others, other solutions to the friend's pain and problems can be found. The friend eventually will be glad to be alive and will someday be glad that you "told."

How Does an Adolescent Deal with Depression and/or Suicidal Feelings When He or She Is Alone?

NOTE TO FACILITATOR:

Opening up a discussion about personal coping skills is sometimes difficult. The whole concept of "coping skills" is probably a new one for young people. Since most young people have pets and use their pets for comfort, talking about pets as a point of reference can be a useful way to facilitate cognition of coping skills. Also, talking about pets is a subject adolescents know a lot about. It allows them in a nonthreatening way to talk about feelings of pain, loss, and rejection and to remember what they have done in the past to help themselves feel better at the time. When they can see that these are "coping skills," they may begin to see how they can draw on such skills over and over again, as well as the importance of developing additional ways to cope.

Is a Dog Useful in Suicide Prevention?

When you are feeling very alone, a wagging tail and a soft warm body wanting to be petted can make you feel pretty good. Feeling needed by a pet for food and affection can also give a person something to live for. The very real value of pets as a resource to help one feel better is written on a well known poster picturing a big yellow cat. "A friend is someone who comes in when the rest of the world goes out." A pet can be a very important resource in helping adults or young people cope with very unhappy periods in their lives.

How Many of You Have Pets? Do Your Pets Ever Help You to Feel Better? How? What Do You Do with Them?

Going for a walk with one's dog can combine two ways to cope. Getting away from the situation that is causing the pain can give one a chance to think and maybe get some perspective. But also, having a pet can provide good company and someone to talk to.

A dog sometimes greets us by jumping and wiggling with joy. How nice it would be to be welcomed by those we love in such a joyous way! Humans are usually a bit more restrained.

How about taking a cat to bed? Hearing that warm reassuring rumble of purring can be a comforting sound. Dogs and cats also absorb tears very well. They don't talk back and disagree with what one says. They are completely nonjudgmental listeners. They don't lecture. They don't give advice. They leave us in control to struggle with our own decisions. Wouldn't it be a treasure to have a friend accept and listen to us that way? Isn't that very special when that happens? Can we learn from what we value about being with our dogs and cats, and somehow translate that into how we treat each other?

What Are Some Other Ways to Cope?

Much emphasis has been placed on how important it is for young people to "reach out" to other people when one is feeling pain, but sometimes other people are not available and ways are needed to cope when one is alone.

Everyone needs to develop personal coping skills. One really needs to develop a long list because sometimes one may try something and it doesn't work so one needs to try something else. Probably, most young people have never thought about the fact that these things one does for one's self are really learned skills. They are things we learn to do to help us, at least temporarily, to deal with unpleasant situations and/or painful feelings. And it surely is healthier to learn how to do certain things to make one feel better than those that are self-destructive. And by self-destructive we're talking about picking on someone else, drinking oneself out of one's mind, running away, driving a car at 90 mph, cutting oneself up with a razor blade.

What Other Things Can One Do When One Is Down? What Do You Do When You're Depressed?

NOTE TO FACILITATOR:
List and discuss possible things to do for oneself and talk about how these activities might help one feel better. When students can share with each other some of their own personal coping strategies, it allows everyone to expand their list of possible things to try when feeling depressed. The list may be far longer than the one here. As a result of this discussion, students may be more actively aware of their own particular coping skills, as well as more fully understanding the logic and necessity for developing such skills. The coping skills that follow will not solve the problem but they may help a person cope while he or she is looking for other solutions. In addition, coping activities which join one with others in learning new skills or sharpening old ones (such as joining a drama club or a volleyball team) can provide a young person with increased feelings of self worth. The adolescent may also find that he or she has renewed pride in him or herself.

1) **Reading a book** allows one to think about something else, perhaps getting a different perspective or finding an escape world in fantasy. One is usually drawn toward reading a book one needs.
2) **Physical exercise**, such as jogging, playing baskets, riding a bike, walking, or dancing, can help one physically release painful feelings. This is somewhat the same as using crying to release pain and anger.
3) **Watching TV or going to the movies** can provide a welcome distraction.
4) **Buying something** may help one feel beautiful when one's self-image is down.
5) **Hobbies** can underscore one's sense of self-worth. Usually, a hobby is an area where one has some expertise. It brings a person joy or the individual would not be drawn to having that particular hobby. For instance, a person might want to join a photography club, or a drama group, a karate class, a choir or band, as a way to

learn and be excited by new skills or contact with other peers who share like interests.

6) **Listening to music** has several values. The sound itself may reinforce what one needs. Powerful music can help a person feel powerful. Gentle music may help an individual to feel stroked. It is also an escape.

7) **Cleaning house or repairing something** allows a person to have something to show for their efforts.

8) **Doing something for someone else** can create a climate where the person can get thanks and strokes at a time when it's hard to ask for what one needs.

9) **Going to a special place** whether that is a special place outside or time alone in one's room can be nourishing simply because one is removed from possible sources of criticism.

Junior High School

DAY III GOALS AND MEANS

GOAL   to support reaching out to other people as a way to cope and listening nonjudgmentally to one another

to provide some hands-on experience in listening awareness skills

MEANS   by developing spontaneous role play situations where young people talk to one another on unconnected telephones

DAY III

Listening Awareness Activity Using Unconnected Telephones/Spontaneous Role Playing Situations

NOTE TO FACILITATOR:
A full description of this activity can be found in Day IV of the Senior High School Program (page 67)

How Does an Adolescent Talk to a Depressed or Suicidal Friend? What Can an Adolescent Say to a Friend Who Has Painful Problems? What Kinds of Questions Does One Ask in Order to Find Out What One's Friend Is Feeling and Experiencing?

Junior high school students are particularly delighted by this activity and usually respond with embarrassed giggles but willingness to experiment.

For junior high school students this activity may be the first time they are made aware of the fact

1) that listening nonjudgmentally and legitimizing another's feelings can be especially supportive to someone who is downcast and struggling with problems. It provides some relief to share one's feelings with another person.

2) that asking open-ended questions may help a friend better understand what he or she is feeling. The listener cannot solve another's problems, but may be able to help the friend clarify them.

Junior High School

DAY IV

OPTIONAL DAY

Parts of the Day V session for Senior High School students are also appropriate for the last day of the Junior High School Program. (See page 79 for a more complete description.)

1) Guest Speaker—Visit to the classroom by a crisis hotline worker or mental health professional to answer "Content questions about teenage suicide." (Question and Answer sheets on pages 82 to 86 and to provide a community concern for adolescents.
2) Discussion and use of "Crisis Cards" (See pages 145-147)
3) Student evaluation of the Living Alternative Program (See pages 70 to 74 in Senior High School Program).

The content test on suicide and depression suggested in the Senior High School Program is less appropriate for Junior High.

ROLE PLAY SCRIPTS

Michael Role Play

Counselor: Suicide Prevention & Crisis Service. Can I help
you?
Student: I don't know. Life's a real bummer.
Counselor: Things haven't been going so well?
Student: They sure haven't. Everyone's getting on my case.
I can't seem to do anything right.
Counselor: With people down on you that can sometimes
make you feel like you're losing at everything.
Student: Yes. You got it! and school . . . Forget it!
Counselor: You sound really discouraged and maybe even a
bit angry.
Student: I just don't care anymore. Well . . . that's not quite
true. I guess I care, but it's not worth it. I'm ready
to hang it up.
Counselor: I get the impression you're feeling pretty trapped
. . . and desperate to change things . . .
Student: You bet I'm desperate! There's no way out of this

one! Nothing is going to change! I can't take it anymore! I just can't take it!

Counselor: You say you can't take it anymore. What has been
going on in your life to make you feel so bad that
you want to (in your words) "Hang it up"?

Student: Mostly, it's my dad. He just yells at me "Do this!
Do that!" and then I do what he tells me to and he
says "You dumb kid! That's a sloppy job! Do it
again and *next time get it right for a change!*"

Counselor: And you feel you've done your best.

Student: Well, I used to try and do a good job, but now
what's the point? It won't matter what I do, I'll just
get yelled at.

Counselor: Did you get yelled at today?

Student: Not today. Yesterday was the last straw. You see
my stepmother sent me to the store to get some
stuff and she doesn't really like me to have the car
alone even though I have my license and I drive really well. I'm a good driver. Anyway, she was desperate for some stuff so she sent me and I was
kinda mad because she was saying "I guess there's
no other way, so you'll have to take the car . . ." It
really bugged me that she was acting like that.

Counselor: Even though she really didn't say it, her attitude
was putting you down.

Student: Yes. And then I blew it! I wasn't thinking I guess. I
was feeling so bad that they don't trust me . . .
They don't trust me! . . . and then when I was backing out, I rammed into a telephone pole. I didn't
see it. The tail-light was busted and a dent in the
trunk. I mean, I felt really sick. I was so sorry . . .
and they just yelled at me . . . how stupid I am . . .
and irresponsible.
So now I'm grounded. I can't go anywhere . . . no
movies, no parties. And to top it off they decided
to punish me for my low grades, too . . . so no
sports until my grades go up.

Counselor: Oh, no . . . No wonder you feel so bummed out.

| | Do you have any friends or people outside of the family that you can talk to and share some of this with in addition to me? |

Student: Well, I sorta have friends but they don't seem to listen. They think I'm too gloomy. They tell me everyone has problems so forget it. We get high sometimes and drink a few and then I don't feel it so much. Do you know a teacher thought I was high one day and he gave me a really hard time and I wasn't even high. I hadn't taken anything. Nobody trusts me. I just want out! And I'm going . . . and nobody is going to stop me.

Counselor: It sounds like you've figured out a way to get out of this situation. Can you tell me what that way is?

Student: What do *you* care?

Counselor: I do care. And from what you've been saying I'm wondering if what you're thinking about, as a way out, is killing yourself?

Student: I might as well! I'm not good at anything. I just get yelled at. I'll make it easy for everyone. They'll probably be glad not to have to bother with me. . . . especially my dad.

Counselor: Have you thought about a way to kill yourself?

Student: I've got some pills. I don't know if it's enough, but I'm sure I can get more.

Counselor: What kind of pills do you have?

Student: I think they're pain-killers. My stepmother has arthritis.

Counselor: I'm really glad you've told me this. I'm pretty sure if we can talk some more, we can come up with some other ways besides killing yourself to deal with all this painful stuff that's going on in your life.

You've really been hurt in many ways, and you're having to face a lot of negative things from home and school and friends, too. It's no wonder you're feeling desperate. It's rough, *really* rough!

Student: It's been awful and I don't know what to do, but

my dad's the worst part. We used to have so much fun together. He'd take me places and we'd talk. But then my parents split (after yelling at each other for a year) and I went to live with my dad. Then *everything changed.*

Counselor: Do you still see your mother?

Student: No. She got married again and moved away. I haven't seen her in a couple of years.

Counselor: So with this divorce you lost both parents. Your mom moved away and your dad seemed to move away in how he treated you. No wonder you feel lonely and rejected. It's not surprising that your school work has been affected. It's pretty hard to study when you're dealing with so much at home. I'm wondering, if you could change one thing right now, what that one thing might be?

Student: I guess I'd like to see my mom. I always liked to be with her. And I don't understand why she doesn't want to see me. I just don't understand it.

Counselor: Does she know you want to see her?

Student: No. I can't tell her that. If she doesn't care, than why should I bother? I think she's moved anyway. I haven't heard from her in a couple of months. Her sister probably knows and she lives in town. I don't know. What's the use?

Counselor: Is your mom's sister someone you can talk to?

Student: I used to. She's really okay. We used to laugh a lot, but I never see her anymore because that makes my dad mad. He didn't like me seeing my mom either.

Counselor: Maybe your aunt misses seeing you, too, and doesn't know that you would like to see her. What would you think of calling her and maybe re-establishing some of that good feeling you two used to have. Maybe you could find out what is going on with your mother. Maybe you'd feel a little less alone . . .

Student: I'd like to see her. I liked her a whole lot. I remember a time when I got into a mess of trouble and she covered for me. I mean it was stupid kid stuff but she was great. She didn't think what I'd done was too cool, but she helped me get through it. After that I used to confide in her a lot and she'd really listen. Maybe I'll call her. I don't care if my dad does get mad. Yes. That's good. Real good.

Counselor: Do you think you could share with her some of these feelings you've told me?

Student: Yes, I think I might be able to do that. I mean if she's like she used to be, I could tell her. Sometimes I think I'm going to explode, or just go crazy. You know, it's been really good talking with you. I feel a lot better.

Counselor: I've liked talking with you, too. I'm wondering how you are feeling now about taking those pills.

Student: Naaa . . . I really feel better. Just getting it out feels like such a relief. And I think I'll make some calls. Maybe I'll call my mother, too. . . .

Karen Role Play

Student: Are you busy right now?

Counselor: No, not particularly. C'mon in. (pause) You look pretty down.

Student: Yeah. I guess I need to talk to someone. It probably won't seem big to you but I don't know what to do.

Counselor: Can you tell me something about it?

Student: Well . . . After school is okay and weekends are okay, but the minute I walk into school I feel really . . . All of my confidence and all of who I think I am . . . just disappears. I feel like I'm blending into the walls of school.

Counselor: Blending into the walls of school? It sounds like becoming invisible. Is invisible what you feel when you're in school, or is it the way you'd like to be?

Student: Both I guess. Most of the time nobody even notices me. For all they care I could be just another brick in the wall. What everyone in this school seems to care about is whether you're wearing designer jeans, or the right sneakers, or wear your hair cut in a flip . . . I don't think I'm doing anything right.

Counselor: What gives you that feeling? I know you say that nobody seems to notice you but how does that mean that you're not doing anything right?

Student: Well . . . It seems like the only time anyone ever does notice me is to put me down. I really wish some one would just give me a chance, wouldn't judge me, or put me down. I wish someone would like me just because I'm me.

Counselor: You'd like a *real friend*. You've been pretty lonely, haven't you.

Student: I don't even want to come to school anymore! And when I'm here I'm not myself. I don't even listen anymore in class and yesterday it was like I was in some sort of haze and I kept falling asleep in class. And, you know there wasn't any reason for me to be tired. And last night I couldn't get to sleep because then I'd have to wake up and come to school. It's like I'm falling into a hole and I don't know where I am or who I am.

Counselor: Did anything particular happen to you yesterday? It seems that yesterday was particularly hard. You know . . . sleeping in class might have been your way of getting away from something and not wanting to come to school today sounds like you didn't want to have to deal with it again.

Student: Well, there was just one more thing to top it off. You know this thing we have in school on Valentine's Day where kids give flowers to someone they like? And the red ones mean I love you and the white ones mean I like you and the pink ones mean I'd like to get to know you. Well, yesterday was Valentine's Day and I sat in home-room and watched the pretty girls and the good looking guys give out all the pretty flowers and they went around and I kept hoping and I knew it was really dumb that I could let the giving of a flower determine if I was a likable person or not but when they went around and skipped me and just kept giving flowers to all of these people and I looked around and saw that one person was liked eight times more than me and another person was liked four times more than me and I had none and to me it was like I was *liked* none . . . I just felt so—like I wasn't even there.

Counselor: Oh, *Karen*! I can really just feel what that must have been like for you.

Student: (nods) It was lonely. I felt *so alone*. (Karen's voice quivers a bit)

Counselor: (reaching out to Karen) All of a sudden it was too much to deal with. You fell asleep in class . . . You didn't want to come to school.

Student: (Karen crying a bit) Yes . . . It just brought it to a head. It was the last straw. Now I feel like I'm the only person who didn't get any flowers though I'm not, but I feel like I'm the only unlikable person in the school. I'm the ugliest brick in the school . . . See part of me feels really different and really alien and part of me doesn't even know who I am . . . (Karen's voice fades out . . .)

FACTORS TO CONSIDER WHEN TALKING WITH DEPRESSED AND/OR SUICIDAL ADOLESCENTS

School administrative personnel, guidance counselors, teachers, youth workers, parents, and young people themselves all come in contact with depressed adolescents. Some of these young people may also be suicidal. This may be frightening to individuals not specifically trained in crisis intervention and not familiar with the dynamics of suicidal feelings. Talking with a depressed young person may evoke in the rescuer feelings of helplessness and fear. "What can I possibly do to relieve this young person's pain? What if I say the wrong thing?" It may be reassuring for a listener to remember that sharing the problems with another person may provide some relief for an adolescent burdened with pain and isolation. *The young person, as a result of sharing his or her feelings, may feel a little less alone.* By having an adult validate the young person's feelings, it may also support the adolescent to feel more in control and relieve feelings of worthlessness or failure. In a sense, what the adult is doing is temporarily helping the young person to hold his/her pain. *In the act of truly accepting the reality of a young person's pain the listener can intensely experience this pain because the adult may truly be hurting for that young person.* In a very real way what has happened is that now the adult is also carrrying these hurts. While this experience can be energy-draining for the listener, for the young person the emotional load may feel less heavy, and he or she may feel a little less desperate.

If, during the course of a personal conversation or in some other interaction with an adolescent, an adult becomes aware of suicidal feelings or thoughts, it is vitally important to intervene. If suicidal feelings exist, it is entirely appropriate to find out from the young person whether he or she has a specific plan for self-destruction, whether the means are at hand for taking his or her life, and whether the individual has set a particular time-frame in which to accomplish this act.

If the danger appears to be imminent, direct action by the inter-vener will relieve the helplessness that a young person is experiencing. Telling the young person exactly what the rescuer intends to do may allow trust to be maintained even though the young person may express some angry ambivalence. A suicidal person is usually very ambivalent about living and dying. There-fore this ambivalence may be expressed in response to rescue. Finally, if there is any reasonably clear immediate threat, arrangements should be made so that the young person is not left alone. Adults are often afraid of over-reacting. One rule of thumb is to *let fear guide you.* If you as rescuer are feeling real fear, then let that fear prompt you into taking some concrete ac-tion. One additional problem may be that parents, out of guilt or their own fear, may deny the rescuer's perceptions and the real-ity of suicidal risk. Contacting a crisis center and/or community emergency outreach service may provide the rescuer with sup-port and help for intervention procedures.

It is true that ultimately one cannot solve another's prob-lems and this may contribute to feelings of ongoing helplessness in a listener or rescuer; however, a listener may be able to help a young person focus on other alternatives in the difficult days ahead.

While listening to adolescents (nonjudgmental concern, problem-solving, and consciousness-raising) can significantly help a young person work through depressive states or crisis sit-uations, it is crucial to realize that suicidal young people need ongoing professional counseling. Since not all therapists will counsel suicidal individuals, it is also important to inquire on this point before making a referral.

Equally important is support for the rescuer(s). Friends, family, and crisis centers can all be used to relieve the burden of responsibility and fear the rescuer(s) might experience as a result of interactions with a suicidal adolescent.

Listed below is a review of the symptoms of a depressive state and/or suicidal behavior. These can be divided into: 1) emotional states, 2) significant life history, 3) behavioral symptoms, and 4) implications of termination behavior.

DEPRESSIVE SYMPTOMATOLOGY AND SUICIDAL STATES

EMOTIONAL STATES

    tension

    self-criticism

    apathy

    feelings of guilt

    sense of hopelessness

    social withdrawal and isolation

    indecisiveness

    sense of helplessness

    feelings of failure

    feeling oneself a burden to others

    preoccupation with unpleasant thoughts (such as death or
        dying)

    ideas of self-punishment

    self-destructive thoughts

    despondency or euphoria

    numb feelings with little or no pleasure from ordinary enjoyable activities and people

    lack of investment in the future and absence of future goal orientation

    exaggerated fear of physical impairments

    inability to express affection, or excessive dependence

Significant Life History (Past and Present)

1. Recent separation from a significant love object.
2. Absence of any warm adult parental figure with whom to identify.
3. Early loss in childhood of a parent through death.
4. History of suicide in the family or others important to adolescent or history of suicidal threats by adolescent.
5. Low communication level with significant others in the environment.
6. Low level of school performance (beneath norm or ability).
7. Active parental conflict and negative attitude expressed toward young person by parent.
8. Lack of control over the environment (defined as little freedom for independent activity due to rigid parental or environmental rules and structure).
9. Child abuse (sexual, physical harm, emotional).
10. Alcoholism of a family member.
11. Battered spouse syndrome is present in the family and young person feels some guilt for the behavior.
12. Divorce or newly reconstituted family with sense of isolation, loss, guilt, or conflict of loyalties.
13. A sensitized fear and hopelessness in the lack of protection by society and/or the outside world to the present and future survival of life, both human and environmental.
14. Unresolved experiences with death.
15. History of failure in personal relationships and/or workplace and/or school.
16. Religious background has been experienced as judgmental or is in conflict with present life style.
17. Stepchild/stepparent conflict.
18. Fear of trusting others due to childhood or adolescent experience where significant others misused power and/or victimized the individual.
19. Inappropriate heavy responsibilities for child-care and housekeeping with no appreciation.

Behavioral Symptoms

loss of appetite

crying spells or inability to cry

listlessness or high activity level

weight loss or weight gain

excessive sleep or insomnia (both with sense of fatigue)

excessive use of drugs or alcohol

sexual promiscuity

truancy or running away

neglect of personal appearance

sudden changes in personality

difficulty in concentration

unusual rebellious behavior

accident proneness

lack of goals or ambitions

writing stories or poems dealing with feelings of personal worthlessness, death, or heaven as a desirable place

drawings that portray morbidity, violence, or self-destructiveness

compulsive joking (the class clown)

inappropriate physical risk-taking

Implications of Termination Behavior

not identifying with any future plans

quietly putting affairs in order

giving away prized possessions

writing some sort of will

verbal clues: "No one will have to worry about me any more."

"I don't want to *be* anything.

"I won't be around to go to that or anything else anymore."

"Maybe I should just kill myself."
"My family would be better off if I was gone."

To help assess the severity of these variables in the four categories, the following questions could be asked about any of the above:

intensity: How intense are the feelings?

duration: How long has this been going on?

frequency: How much of the time is the person feeling this way?

In assessment, the greater the intensity, the longer the emotional state and/or situation has lasted, the frequency with which the person is dealing with negative feelings within a single day are valuable indicators as to whether there is a need for speed in intervention.

Finally, it is the total picture that needs examination. If an adolescent is feeling severe tension and self-criticism for good reasons, but appears to have reasonable control over his or her emotional state, the young person probably could benefit from counseling but may not exhibit suicidal behavior.

Successful prevention, however, is working with an adolescent so as to help him/her deal with problematic situations before the young person's coping strategies and/or emotional state have deteriorated to the point where a last-straw event could trigger a suicidal act.

Specific Factors to Consider When Dealing with Depressed or Suicidal Adolescents

The suicidal feelings of an adolescent are the same as for an adult: low self-esteem and feelings of worthlessness, deep depression accompanied by an overwhelming sense of hopelessness and helplessness.

However, the confusing and transitional nature of being an adolescent creates a further need for understanding adolescence itself in order to deal more effectively with an adolescent's suicidal feelings.

1. An adolescent is a person who is trying to grow up but sometimes gets very confused and/or scared and slips back into the security of being a child.

2. An adolescent usually tries very hard to be responsible and independent, but usually doesn't have a backlog of enough personal experience to carry through to the satisfaction of most adults.

3. Adolescents are people who vividly notice when there is a discrepancy between the rules and values espoused by adults and adult behavior.

4. Adolescents are people who have the same intense emotional needs and feelings as adults but little understanding of how to recognize or cope with these emotions.

5. Adolescents are trying to figure out who they are now and who they want to be. They are particularly vulnerable to feeling a sense of their own worthlessness as a person.

6. Adolescents have a strong need to try out walking on their own, but they need a secure base to fall back on. With the increasing disorganization and breakdown in traditional family life, high rates of unemployment, enormous school pressures, competition for success, and peer pressure, many young people feel as if they are rocking in a boat that has no anchor.

7. Because of negative childhood experiences, some adolescents early on have written off adults as resources and place a high value on peer relationships. But when the peer group does not take the adolescent seriously, or is not available to them, and when they haven't made a good connection with family members or other adults, they are really adrift.

8. Most adolescents have not formed a cohesive value system that would support them in what to live *for*, so

even this tremendously important anchor of security is often not yet within their grasp.

9. Adolescents are locked into financial and emotional dependence on their families. When the family situation does not feel nurturing or supportive, the adolescent has very few options and may in actuality be truly trapped and helpless, unless he or she can not only express personal needs but have these needs taken seriously.

   In addition to being a "cry for help," an adolescent suicide attempt may be a "scream for change."

10. Often, adolescents have trouble identifying the underlying causes for their depression. They only know they feel terrible and they don't know what to do. Previously, they may have acted out their pain by getting into trouble at school, with the law, by running away, trying drugs, alcohol, promiscuity; or they may have quietly faded into the wall, convinced that everybody picks on them and nobody is their friend.

    Alienation and isolation from significant others increase because they fear that in admitting their confusion and pain, they will not be considered grown up or they are afraid they will be rejected.

11. Sometimes what adolescents need to talk about involves violating family secrets which they may find terribly hard to do because revelation creates uncomfortable feelings of disloyalty and guilt or fears of retribution and rejection from the family. Not being able to discuss family problems increases the young person's isolation, an important factor in the development of suicidal feelings.

Listening to Adolescents

Empathic listening, reflecting the adolescent's feelings, supporting and exploring possible options are techniques which are as valuable to use with adolescents as with adults. However, adolescents, particularly thirteen and fourteen year olds, are more accustomed to being talked at than listened to. Adults find it terribly easy to proffer "what to do." The temptation to give advice becomes even more seductive when a teenager is feeling quite desperate about a problem that may seem quite easy to solve from the adults' point of view. However, as in working with adults, giving advice can be a real trap. If the advice doesn't work, the young person can blame an adult rather than looking for other, perhaps more realistic reasons. If the advice does work, the individual may not see the success as his or her own.

A more valuable approach is educating the adolescent. Usually adolescents do not have a backlog of experience for understanding their emotions or the problems they are facing. Helping young people understand and name their emotions, and clarifying why they feel the way they do can be extremely useful. For too many adolescents, no one has ever taken the time to listen seriously or legitimize their feelings. Sometimes an adolescent will exaggerate a problem simply because his or her experience has taught that if the problem isn't dramatic enough, adults will simply pass it off. Adolescents often need from an adult a reality test that what is happening or what they are experiencing is legitimate in itself without the need for exaggeration.

Not taking a young person's feelings seriously fosters defensiveness rather than openness. What is sometimes forgotten is that adolescents feel with the same intensity as adults. The loss of a pet, or a friend moving away may seem rather trivial to an adult dealing with loss of a spouse or job; however, the pain levels can be equivalent. Also, it is useful to keep in mind that the apparently minor loss may only be the tip of the iceberg or the last straw for a young person. It is possible that the adolescent doesn't even realize that the real problems aren't the ones he or she is talking about. John Mack and Holly Hickler in their ground-breaking book *VIVIENE, The Life and Suicide of an Adolescent Girl*, analyze the peculiar complexity of the adolescent suicide. It is their analysis that "the actual decision to kill oneself, although it may have been incubating for months or even years, is, nevertheless, strongly affected by the situation that immediately precedes the suicidal act."[1]

The pendulum between life and death can swing very delicately for an adolescent, who in maturational development is already very prone to dramatic moodswings. An apparently minor situation such as an argument with a parent, name-calling by peers, or a failed school quiz can precipitate a suicidal act.

However, if the problem does turn out to be a minor loss with no underlying layers of pain, it is still important to take the young person's feelings seriously. If the young person learns how to cope with and work through minor losses, he or she may be taking a giant step toward learning how to cope with other losses faced later in life.

Also, thoughtful listening to a young person's problems and feelings can prevent further deterioration into suicidal behavior; however, getting a fair and accurate reading of an adolescent's feelings about a situation can be difficult. Adolescents tend to be very private about their inner thoughts and struggles, perhaps because at this age they are not yet sure how to put together the pieces of their inner self into a workable whole. Life still represents for them a puzzle.

Interestingly enough, Dr. John Coleman (1980) in *The Nature of Adolescence* characterizes the adolescent period as a time when the young person needs to mourn adequately the loss of childhood in order to put it aside and fully move into adult life. If one thinks about leaving childhood as a loss to be mourned, one can perhaps be more sensitive to the dramatic behavior shifts that often accompany adolescent growth.

This concept is particularly apt when applied to adolescents who have been overly sheltered and protected from taking responsibility. Open rebellion against parents is often in direct proportion to the degree of shelter the adolescent has experienced in the family. Great negativity is sometimes a posture that masks heavy dependence. Negativity gets a lot of attention from parents. It keeps the adolescent in overt contact with them. At

---

[1]Mack, J. E. & Hickler, H. *Viviene, The life and suicide of an adolescent girl.* Boston: Little, Brown & Company, 1981, p. 195.

the same time, this rebellion is a young person's attempt to get a sense of independence and separation from childhood. If adults understand that rebellion may be a conflict within the adolescent, and that the leaving of childhood may represent a significant loss, they may be less prone to be so punitive toward the young person who backslides into childish irresponsibility. Parents may look for other ways to help an adolescent learn from those irresponsible moments.

Conversely, parents may have some real ambivalence themselves about allowing the dependent child to become an independent adult. The adolescent growing into full adulthood may represent a similar loss for the parent. The parent, while welcoming less responsibility, may feel less needed. "Daddy's little girl" and "Mama's boy" represent the extremes of not allowing the natural transition from teenager into adulthood.

The attitude of "You should know better" can seriously hamper parent/offspring communication at a time when good communication is especially needed. Not wishing to appear as a child who can be punished, the adolescent may not feel free to share his/her fears or failures with parents. The inability to share deep feelings represents another significant loss for the adolescent. If the parent is not able to share feelings of loss and ambivalence over the young person's growth to adulthood, both parent and adolescent experience loss. As adult models we need to be sensitive to both adolescent and parent. Out-of-family adults who talk with adolescents can perform a significant educational function by clarifying these family dynamics.

ADDITIONAL RESOURCES

Coleman, J.C. *The nature of adolescence*. London & New York: Methuen, 1980.

Faucher, E. *Surviving*. New York: Scholastic Inc., 1985.

Francke, L.B. *Growing up divorced*. New York: Linden Press/Simon & Schuster, 1983.

Giovacchini, P. *The urge to die: Why young people commit suicide*. New York: Macmillan Publishing Co., 1981.

Hoff, L.A. *People in crisis*. Menlo Park, CA: Addison-Wesley Publishing Co., 1983.

Klagsbrun, F. *Too young to die*. New York: Pocket Books, 1981.

Krementz, J. *How it feels when a parent dies*. New York: Alfred A. Knopf, Inc., 1981.

LeShan, E. *Learning to say goodbye when a parent dies*. New York: Avon Books, 1978.

Mack, J.E. & Hickler, H. *Vivienne*. Boston: Little, Brown, & Co., 1981.

McCay, K. & Wibbelsman, C. *The teenage body book*. New York: Pocket Books, 1978.

Rabkin, B. *Growing up dead*. Nashville: Abingdon, 1978.

Sgroi, S.M. *Handbook of clinical intervention in child sexual abuse.* Lexington, MA: Lexington Books, 1982.

FILMS:

Teenage Suicide: *But Jack Was a Good Driver*, 16mm
Code 106666-7
CRM McGraw-Hill Films
110 Fifteenth Street
Del Mar, CA

Urgent Messages, 16mm
Laser Educational Media Society
Gary Mavis, R.S.W.
Executive Director
Crisis Intervention & Suicide Prevention Centre
1946 West Broadway
Vancouver, BC

ABOUT THE AUTHOR

In 1979 Polly Joan joined Suicide Prevention & Crisis Service of Tompkins County, New York, with a mandate to develop an Adolescent Outreach Program in suicide prevention and crisis intervention.

As coordinator, she has spearheaded Program Development both in the school system and community in order to stem the rise of adolescent suicide. As well as working with school systems to provide education in suicide prevention, and supervising an innovative crisis counseling program for adolescents in local high schools, Polly Joan provides training for a range of workshops focusing on crisis counseling, intervention management, and assessment of suicidal risk in order to meet the professional needs local communities face in dealing with today's "at risk" adolescent.

For consultation in Program Development or Training Workshops, Polly Joan may be contacted through TFC ASSOCIATES, 604 Taylor Place, Ithaca, New York 14850.

"CRISIS CARDS" AS HANDOUTS FOR ADOLESCENTS

"Crisis Cards" provide a practical, everyday reminder to adolescents. The cards list warning signs that an emergency may be coming, some of the myths and facts about adolescent suicide, and local telephone numbers to call in the event of a crisis. To have these cards in their wallets or posted near a phone provides a measure of security for young people. It helps the adolescent feel less trapped and more in control.

A school system might find printing "crisis cards" a viable prevention expense. Other possible funding sources might be through United Way/Community Chest, a community mental health agency, a crisis hotline and/or suicide prevention service.

Sample card used by Suicide Prevention & Crisis Service of Tompkins County, New York.

WARNING SIGNS THAT AN EMERGENCY MAY BE COMING . . .

* Major loss (of loved person, home, possessions, or status), especially if preceded by other losses.
* Neglect of appearance.
* Unusual change in school work or attendance.
* Withdrawal from people, especially close friends.
* Insomnia or oversleeping; weight loss or gain.
* Putting oneself down.
* Self-injury.
* Staying away or running away from home.

* Irritability and restlessness.
* Angry outbursts at home or school.
* Use of alcohol or drugs as an escape from pain.
* Sudden beginning of self-destructive or risk-taking behavior, like fast driving.
* Intense feelings of being trapped and helpless, without any hope of changing the situation.
* Specific threats of suicide (verbal or written).
* Prior suicide attempts.
* Giving away prized possessions.

Trust your feelings. If you sense that something is wrong, it probably is.

WHAT TO DO

* Listen and show that you care.

* If you suspect suicidal thoughts, don't be afraid to talk openly with the person. You will not cause more trouble, or give the person ideas, by asking about suicide.

    Is there a specific plan? Have any steps been taken to carry out the plan? Does the person have any friends or family who are supportive? . . .The fewer supports and the more specific the plan, the greater the suicidal risk.

* Stay with the person if you feel there is any danger.

* **Get help from a trusted adult or Suicide Prevention & Crisis Service. 272-1616**

SURVIVAL

I cannot fly into that prism of colors
letting myself fragment
into a thousand sensual pieces
unless I know
I can pick up the shards
and put them back into the oneness
of me
because selfhood is all
I can count on

Polly Joan

INDEX